FIRST 50 CHORD PROGRESSIONS

YOU SHOULD PLAY ON PIANO

by Mark Harrison

To access audio, visit:
www.halleonard.com/mylibrary

Enter Code
1125-2625-3920-6282

ISBN 978-1-7051-8069-3

Visit Hal Leonard Online at
www.halleonard.com

World headquarters, contact:
Hal Leonard
7777 West Bluemound Road
Milwaukee, WI 53213
Email: info@halleonard.com

In Europe, contact:
Hal Leonard Europe Limited
Dettingen Way
Bury St Edmunds, Suffolk, IP33 3YB
Email: info@halleonardeurope.com

In Australia, contact:
Hal Leonard Australia Pty. Ltd.
4 Lentara Court
Cheltenham, Victoria, 3192 Australia
Email: info@halleonard.com.au

CONTENTS

INTRODUCTION

Welcome to *First 50 Chord Progressions You Should Play on Piano*. This book will show you how to play the most common chord progressions found in great popular songs. Along the way, you'll also learn how to stylize your chord progressions so your playing sounds authentic, just like on your favorite recordings!

We've organized the progressions into sections, beginning with simpler pop and rock progressions featuring two or three chords and finishing with more advanced combinations found in R&B, jazz, and blues music. Each chord progression comes with two playing examples; the first notates a basic spelling of each chord, while the second shows how to play that progression in a popular-music style. Song references are provided for each progression, allowing you to reference what you've learned to the music you love.

You'll notice that all the music in this book includes numbers by the notes. This guidance suggests finger numbers you could use to play the chords.

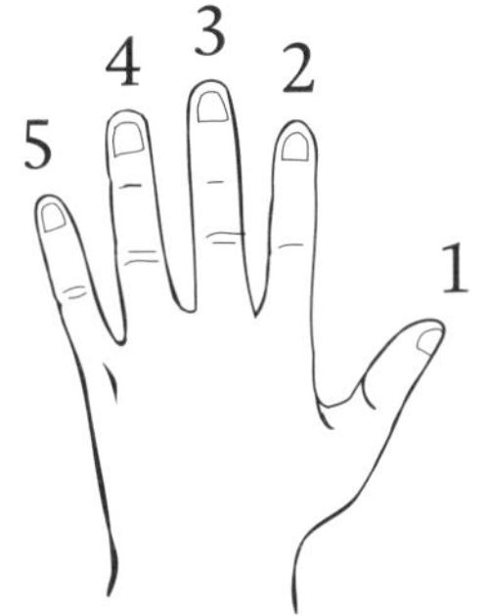

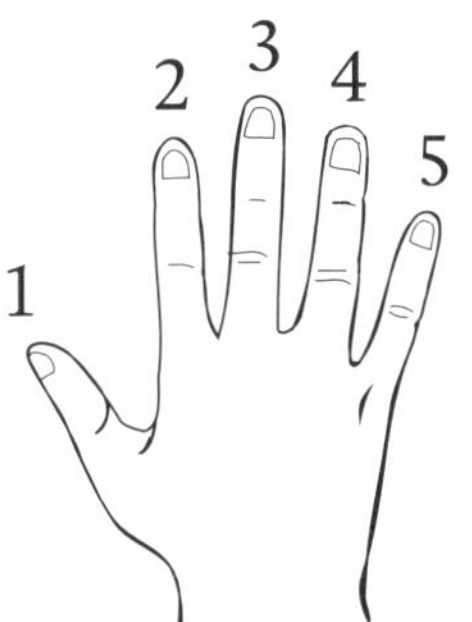

ABOUT THE AUDIO

The price of this book includes exclusive online recordings to help you get playing faster than ever before!

Each of the 50 chord progressions in this book comes with two audio tracks. The first is a "basic chords" solo piano demonstration, where you can hear the progressions played in their most simple, easy-to-follow form. The second is a "Rhythmic Style" track, showing how to play the chord progression in a particular musical style. Here, the piano interpretation of the progression is on the right channel and a backing band is on the left channel. To play along with the band on these tracks, just turn down the right channel. Audio tracks are preceded by a "count-in" of clicks to help set the speed of the beat.

To access audio, simply go to www.halleonard.com/mylibrary and enter the unique code found on page 1 of this book. This will grant you instant access to every file. You can download to your computer, tablet, or phone, or stream live.

PROGRESSIONS WITH TWO CHORDS

PROGRESSION 1

Song Reference: "Achy Breaky Heart (Don't Tell My Heart)" by Billy Ray Cyrus

Progression Tip: Most common two-chord progressions use some combination of chords I (one), IV (four), and/or V (five) from the key of the song. (E.g., in the key of A these are chords A, D, and E.) Because each chord contains three different notes, it is called a **triad**. A triad comprises the **root** note (after which the chord is named, e.g., "A"), the **third** above the root, and the **fifth** above the root. These notes are distributed between right and left hands, with some notes appearing more than once. Here, we are going to use chords I and V in the key of A.

Basic Progression

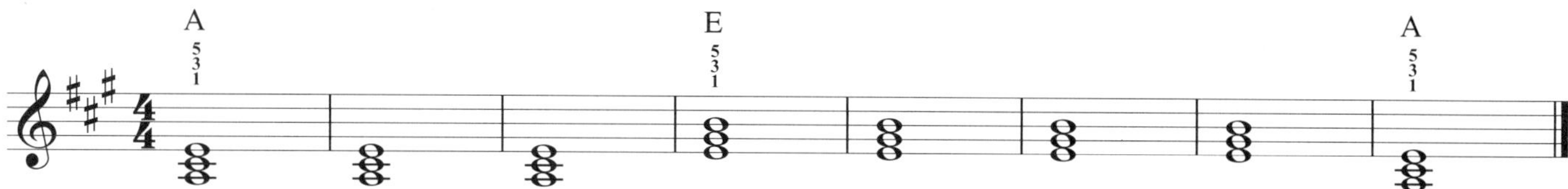

Rhythmic Style: Country-Pop

PROGRESSION 2

Song Reference: "Born in the U.S.A." by Bruce Springsteen

Progression Tip: You'll have noticed the "Rhythmic Style" music in the last progression reordered (**inverted**) some of the triad notes in the right hand. This is called **voice leading** and makes the progressions sound smoother. We'll also be doing that in this progression, which moves between chords I and IV in the key of B.

Basic Progression

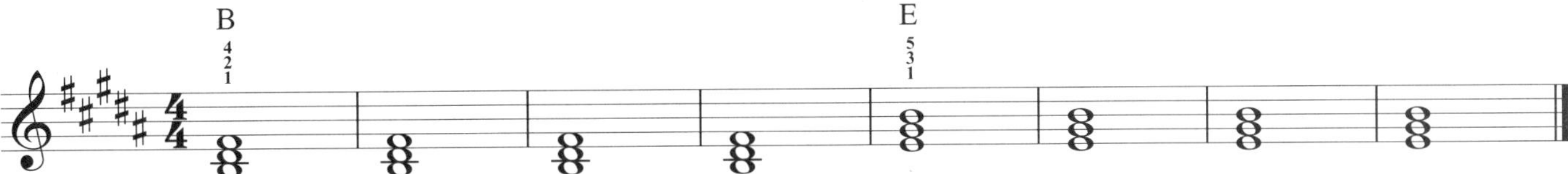

Rhythmic Style: Pop/Rock

PROGRESSION 3

Song Reference: "I Still Haven't Found What I'm Looking For" by U2

Progression Tip: This progression also uses chords I and IV, now in C. Like the last "Rhythmic Style," this one contains some notes that lie outside of the basic triad (**non-chord tones**). These add movement and interest to the progression.

Basic Progression

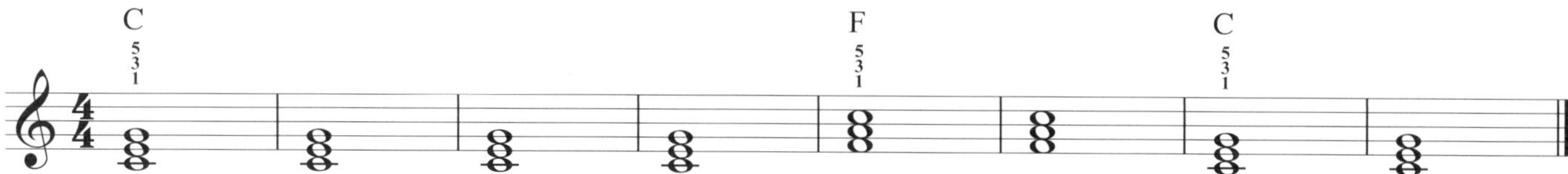

Rhythmic Style: Classic Rock

PROGRESSION 4

Song Reference: "Stop Whispering" by Radiohead

Progression Tip: Here, we are using the sustain pedal to create a more continuous sound effect. Be sure to release the pedal at the point of each chord change. Some of the triads are **octave doubled**. This means the top note is played twice at different octaves for a bit more power.

Basic Progression

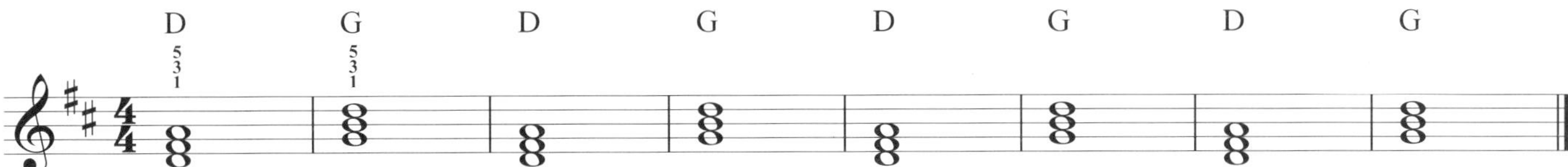

Rhythmic Style: Pop-Rock

PROGRESSION 5

Song Reference: "You Never Can Tell" by Chuck Berry

Progression Tip: We are playing more non-chord tones, here. With this chord progression they are found in the middle of the chord, and in both hands. This **interior movement** is particularly popular in rock styles of the 1950s.

Basic Progression

Rhythmic Style: Rock 'n' Roll

PROGRESSIONS WITH THREE CHORDS

PROGRESSION 6

Song Reference: "The First Cut Is the Deepest" by Sheryl Crow

Progression Tip: This is a basic three-chord progression, combining all the chords we've looked at so far (I, IV, and V).

Basic Progression

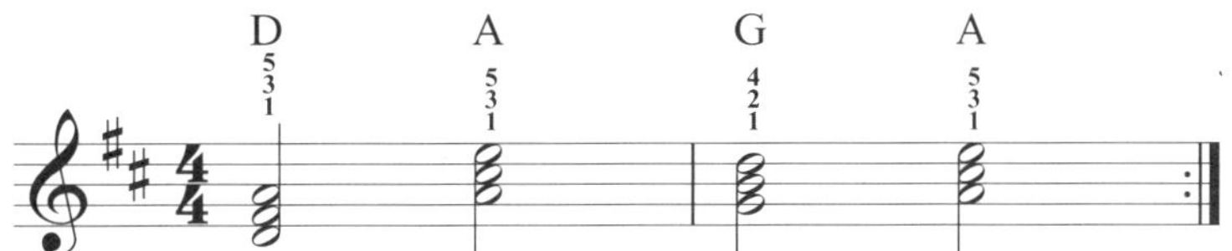

Rhythmic Style: Rock Ballad

D A G A D A

Ped. Ped. sim.

G A D A

G A D A G A

PROGRESSION 7

Song Reference: "Mr. Jones" by Counting Crows

Progression Tip: Here, we are using our basic I, IV, and V chords but in the key of C (using the chords of C, F, and G). Typically in our "Rhythmic Style" music, the right hand plays all the notes of the triad. The left hand plays the root, with some thumb rhythms (sometimes on the fifth) for a bit of drive.

Basic Progression

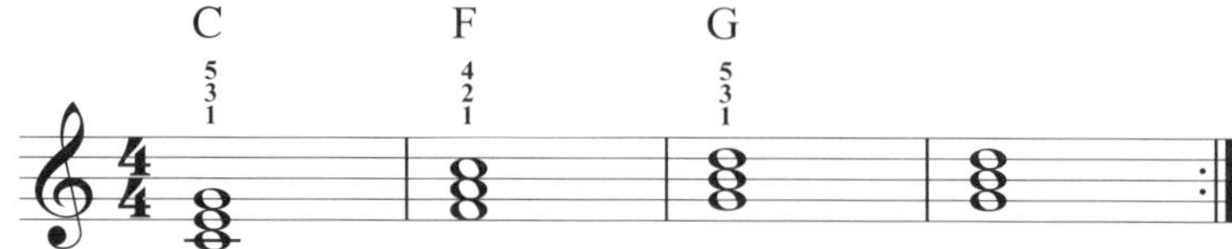

Rhythmic Style: Pop/Rock

C F G

Ped. Ped. sim.

C F G

C F G

C F G

PROGRESSION 8

Song Reference: "Wild Thing" by The Troggs

Progression Tip: This progression moves through chords I–IV–V–IV in D. Notice how both hands play the exact same rhythm in the "Rhythmic Style" music. This is known as **concerted** rhythms.

Basic Progression

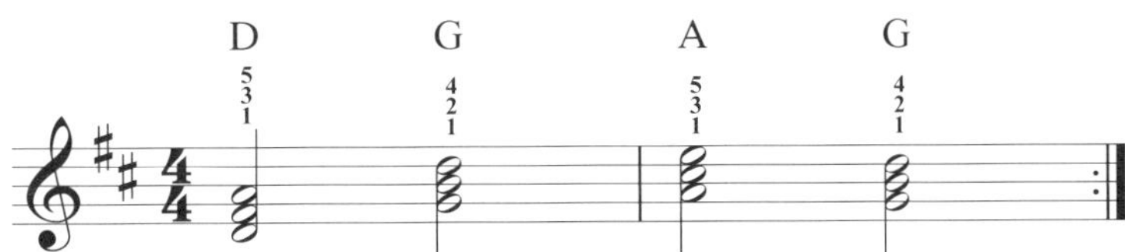

Rhythmic Style: Rock (1960s)

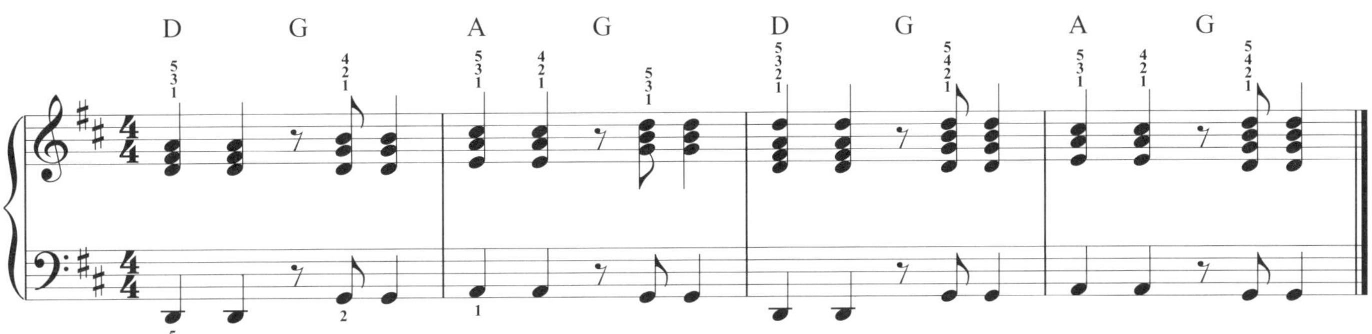

PROGRESSION 9

Song Reference: "Drops of Jupiter (Tell Me)" by Train

Progression Tip: The **root** of each chord is the lowest left-hand note. We're using **inversions** of the right-hand triads to **voice lead** between chords. This means mixing up the basic triad note order, allowing for smoother movement.

Basic Progression

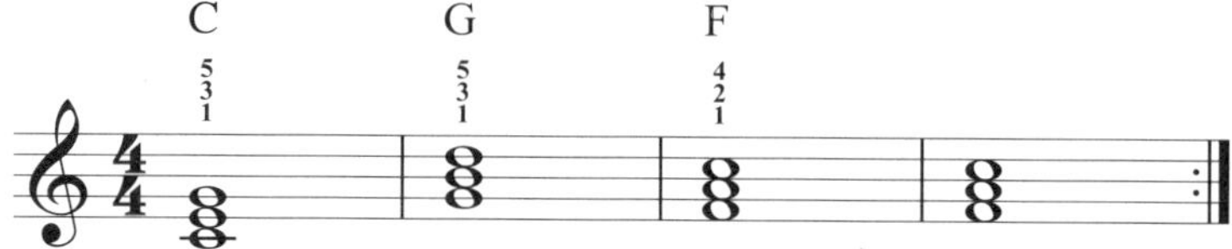

Rhythmic Style: Modern Rock

PROGRESSION 10

Song Reference: "American Idiot" by Green Day

Progression Tip: Here, we are using chords I, IV, and V in the key of A-flat major. The "Rhythmic Style" progression is a useful example of the upbeat piano style used to accompany pop and punk genres (known as **comping**).

Basic Progression

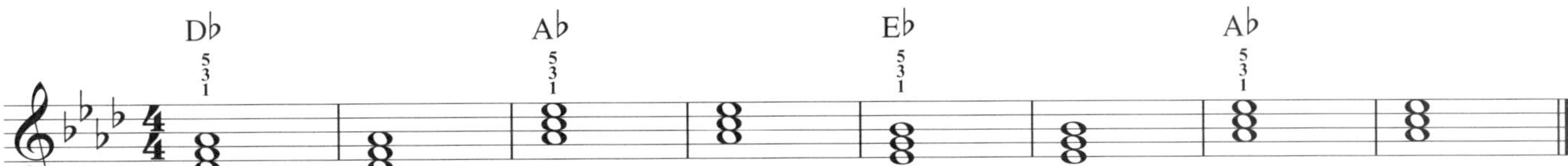

Rhythmic Style: Up Tempo Pop-Punk

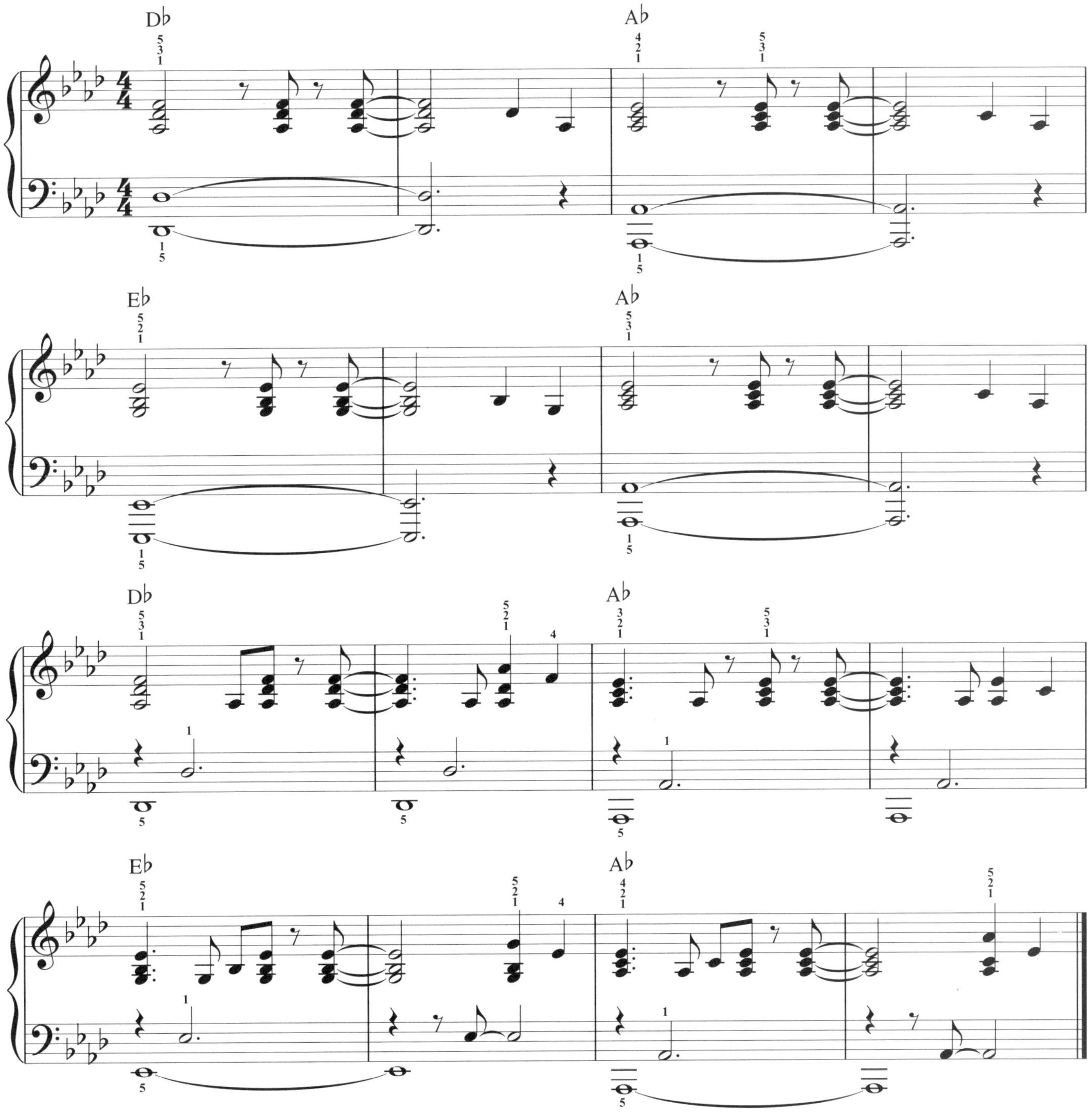

PROGRESSIONS WITH FOUR CHORDS

PROGRESSION 11

Song Reference: "With or Without You" by U2

Progression Tip: This chord progression contains four different chords. The additional one is chord vi (six). This is our first **minor** chord. Minor chords sound darker, so this adds a bit of intensity to the progression. Up to this point, we've only been playing **major**, happier-sounding chords.

Basic Progression

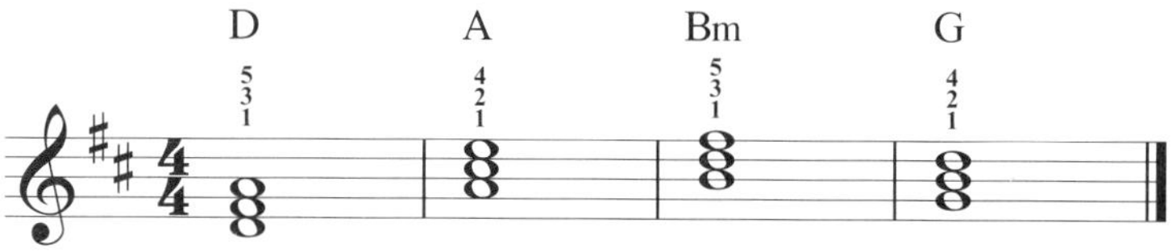

Rhythmic Style: Rock

PROGRESSION 12

Song Reference: "Poker Face" by Lady Gaga

Progression Tip: We're in the key of B major, here. This means we have quite a few black keys to play, so take your time to learn the basic progression carefully. In this key, the minor vi chord is G-sharp minor.

Basic Progression

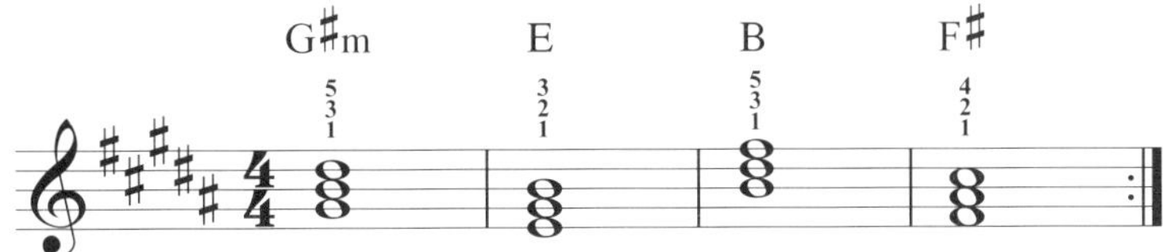

Rhythmic Style: Modern Pop

PROGRESSION 13

Song Reference: "Crocodile Rock" by Elton John

Progression Tip: In this chord progression, the minor vi chord is E minor. Even though this chord gives our progression a mix of minor and major sounds, the music remains **diatonic**. This means it uses notes that belong to the key. You can tell this because there are no additional sharp, flat, or natural symbols by the noteheads.

PROGRESSION 14

Song Reference: "What Ya Want from Me" by Adam Lambert

Progression Tip: Take time to practice the "Rhythmic Style" slowly and carefully. Here, the right-hand chords are landing a sixteenth-note before the main beat. This **anticipation** is tricky but a great tool for sounding like an authentic player of R&B and rock styles.

Basic Progression

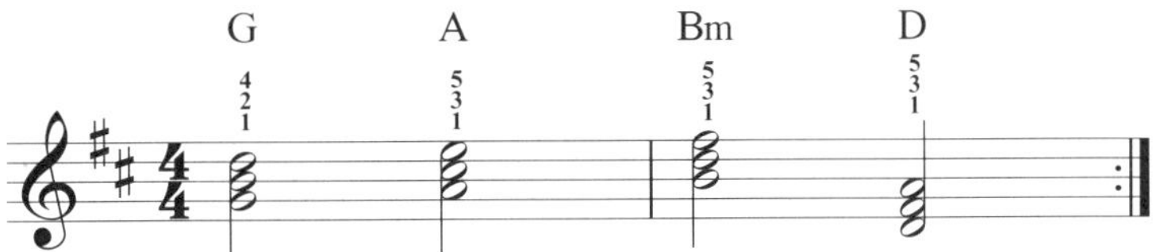

Rhythmic Style: Modern Rock

G A Bm D G A

Bm D G A Bm D

G A Bm D

PROGRESSION 15

Song Reference: "She Drives Me Crazy" by Fine Young Cannibals

Progression Tip: Here, the "Rhythmic Style" music gives you a great example of simple pop-piano playing using four chords in D major: I (D), IV (G), vi (Bm), and V (A).

Basic Progression

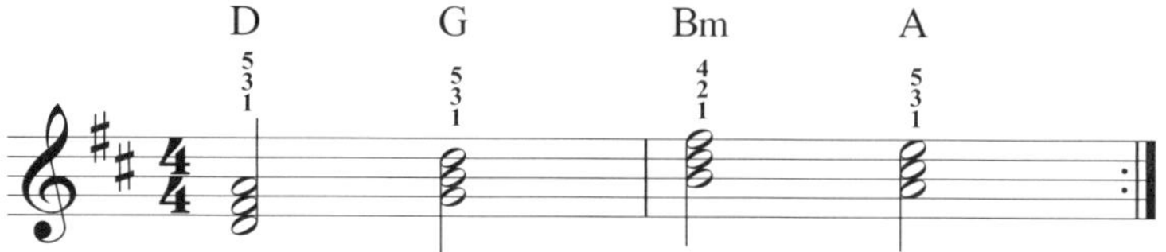

Rhythmic Style: Classic Pop

PROGRESSION 16

Song Reference: "Just Can't Get Enough" by Black Eyed Peas

Progression Tip: This progression begins with chord vi (C minor) in the key of E-flat major. The "Rhythmic Style" music for this four-chord progression gets progressively busier, with increasing numbers of shorter note values in a hip-hop groove.

Basic Progression

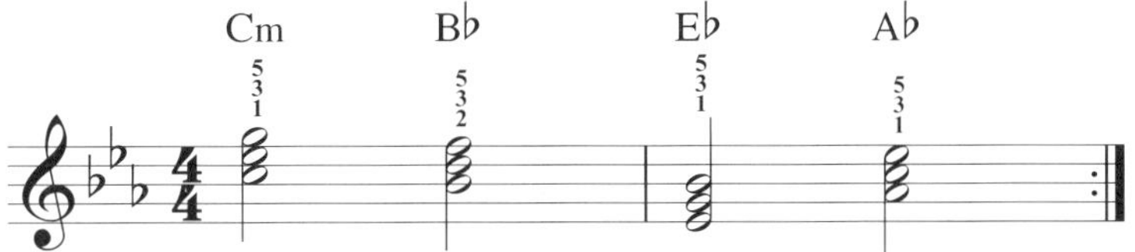

Rhythmic Style: Hip Hop

PROGRESSIONS WITH SIX CHORDS

PROGRESSION 17

Song Reference: "Tears in Heaven" by Eric Clapton

Progression Tip: From now on, we're going to add two more chords to our progressions: chords ii (two) and iii (three). Both are minor chords. We'll also add two more playing techniques. The first involves **bass inversions**, where a note other than the root is lowest in the left hand. (You'll see this written using a slash in the chord symbol. So, "A/C♯" means an A chord but with "C-sharp" in the left-hand bass.) We'll also be using **suspended triads**. This is where the normal third of the chord is replaced by a note four steps above the root. (E.g., an "Esus4" chord now has the notes E, **A**, and B.)

Basic Progression

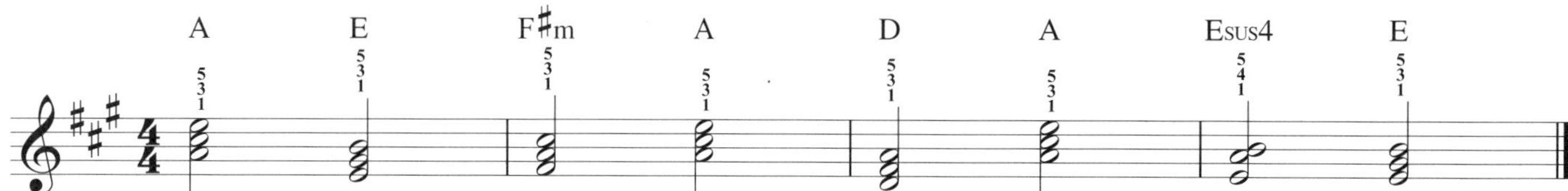

Rhythmic Style: Pop Ballad

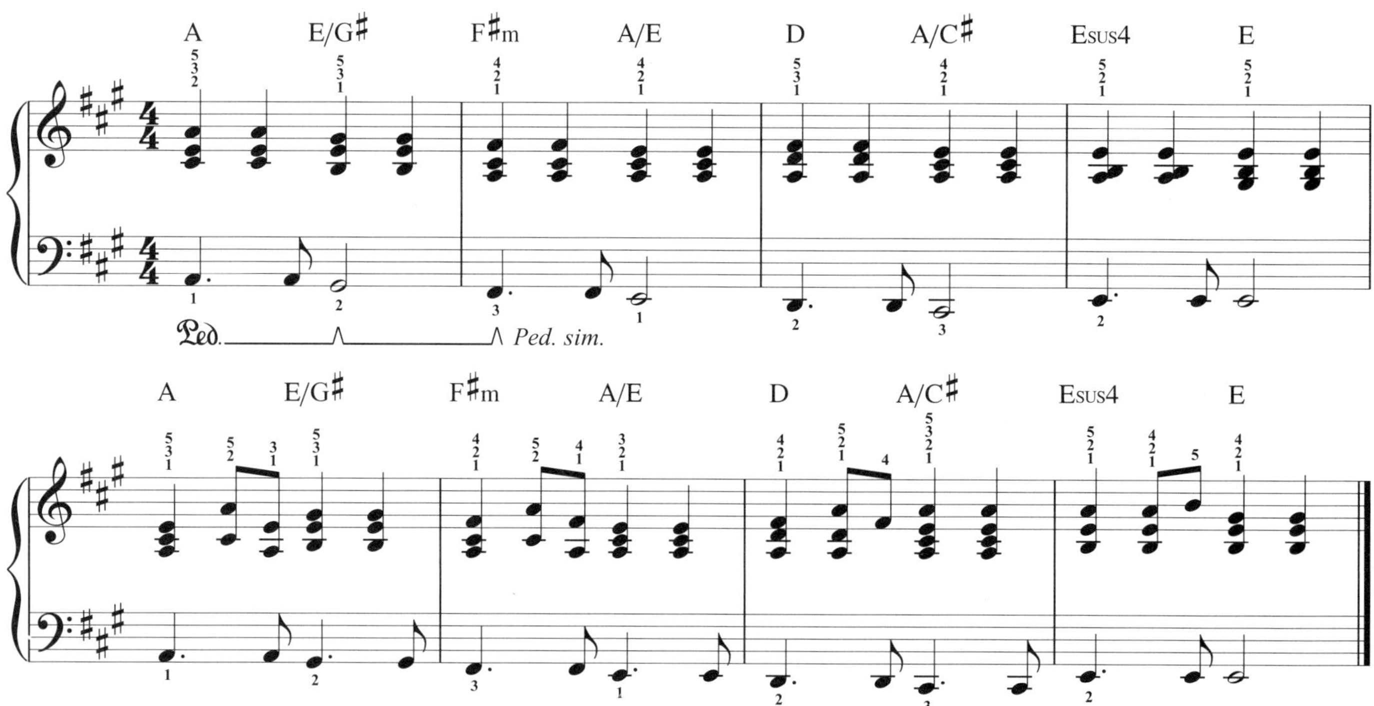

PROGRESSION 18

Song Reference: "A Whiter Shade of Pale" by Procol Harum

Progression Tip: Because we are in the major key of C, our three minor chords in this progression are D minor (ii), E minor (iii), and A minor (vi). In the "Rhythmic Style" music some of our bass inversions use non-chord tones, too.

Basic Progression

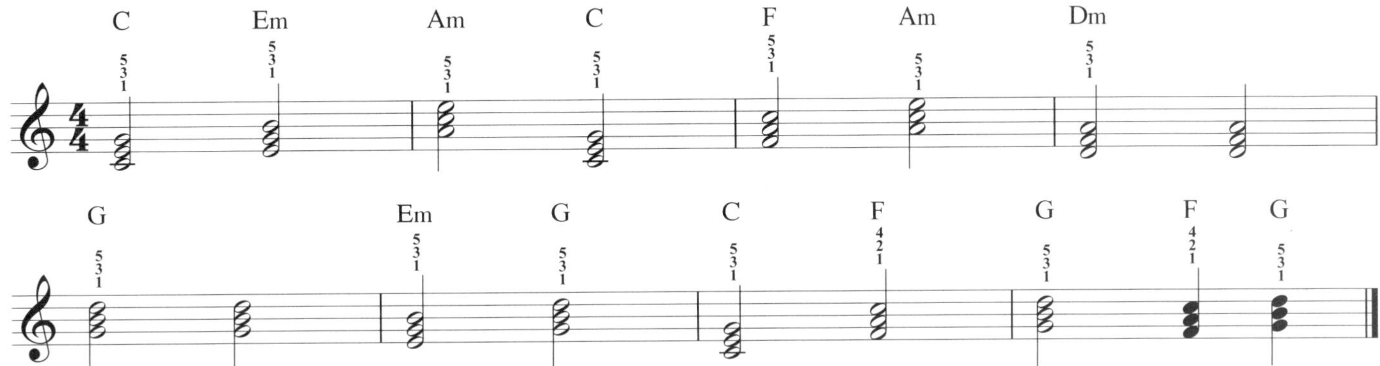

Rhythmic Style: Classic Pop

PROGRESSION 19

Song Reference: "When a Man Loves a Woman" by Percy Sledge

Progression Tip: Here, we use the term "triplet feel" when the quarter-note pulse is divided into three equal parts (see the triplet "3" sign used in the "Rhythmic Style" music). This example could also have been notated in 12/8 time. Our progression travels through chords I-V-vi-iii-IV-V-I-V in D-flat major.

Basic Progression

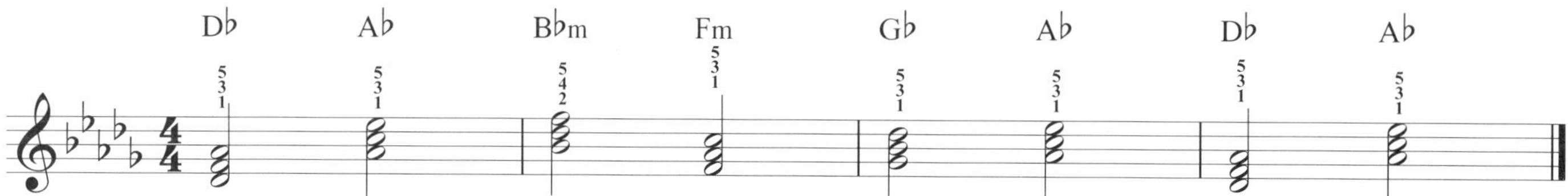

Rhythmic Style: Ballad

PROGRESSION 20

Song Reference: "Goodbye Yellow Brick Road" by Elton John

Progression Tip: The "Rhythmic Style" music for this progression contains another example of non-chord tones used within a bass inversion, to smoothen out the line. Rhythmic values become shorter as the music progresses, giving a sense of momentum.

Basic Progression

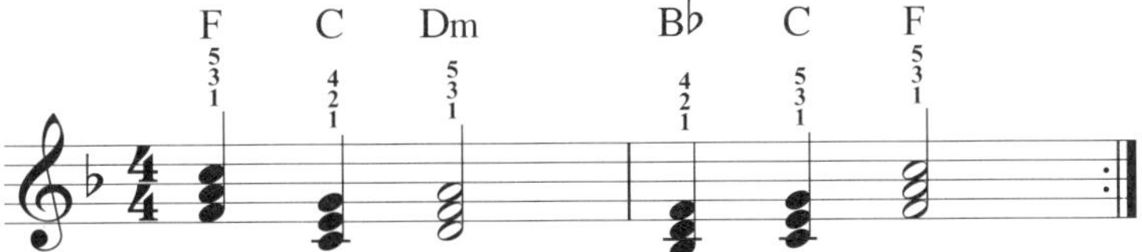

Rhythmic Style: Pop Ballad

PROGRESSIONS IN MINOR KEYS

PROGRESSION 21

Song Reference: "Rolling in the Deep" by Adele

Progression Tip: Up to this point, we've been playing chords in the context of major keys. So, while some of the chords (e.g., chord vi) were minor, all of the chords belonged to the major scale and key of the progression. Here in a minor key progression, all of the chords are found in the corresponding minor scale and key. We'll also be using the ♭VII (flat seven) chord in this progression for the first time. In the key of C minor, this is a B-flat major chord.

Basic Progression

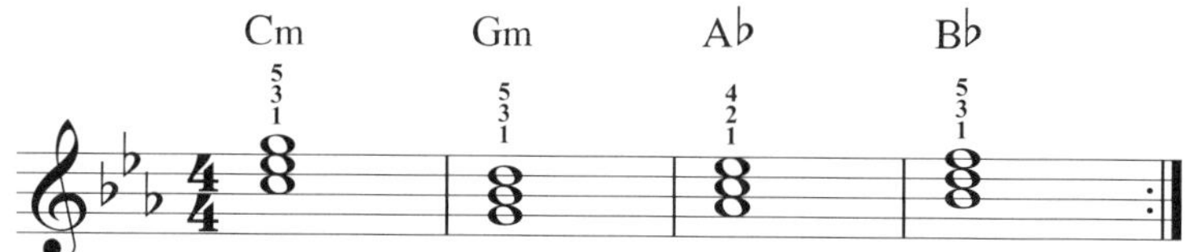

Rhythmic Style: Modern Pop

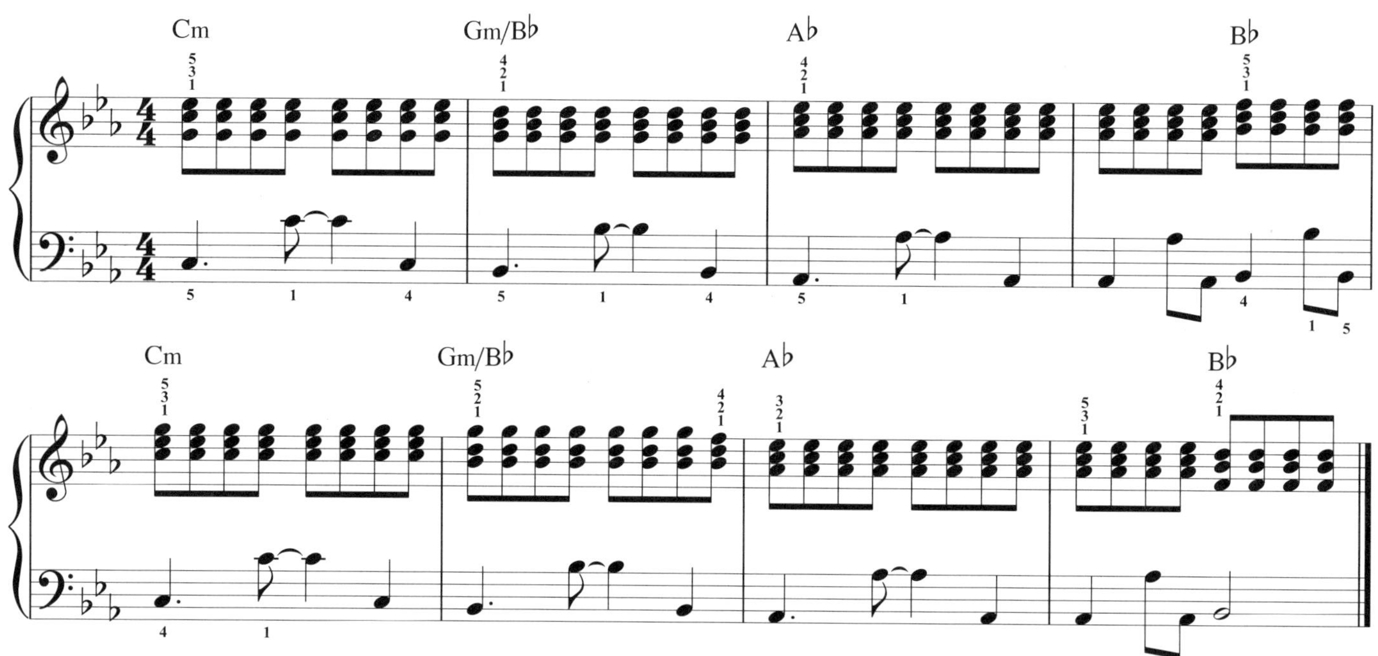

PROGRESSION 22

Song Reference: "Livin' on a Prayer" by Bon Jovi

Progression Tip: This E minor progression uses the ♭VII chord again (D), in both regular and "sus" form. The "Rhythmic Style" music sometimes only use two notes of the right-hand triad: the root and the fifth. This is a chord-playing technique common to many rock styles.

Basic Progression

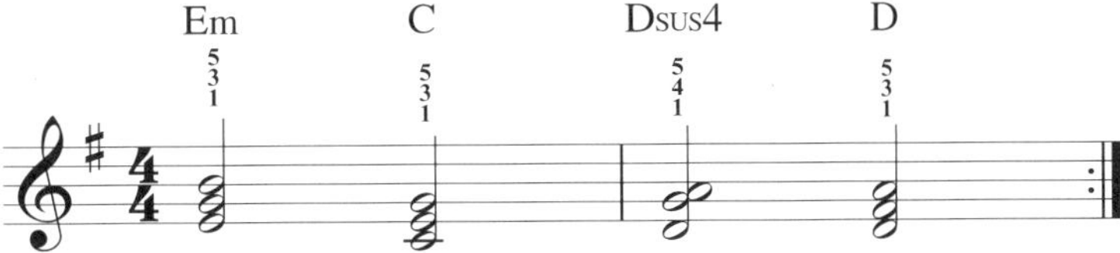

Rhythmic Style: Rock

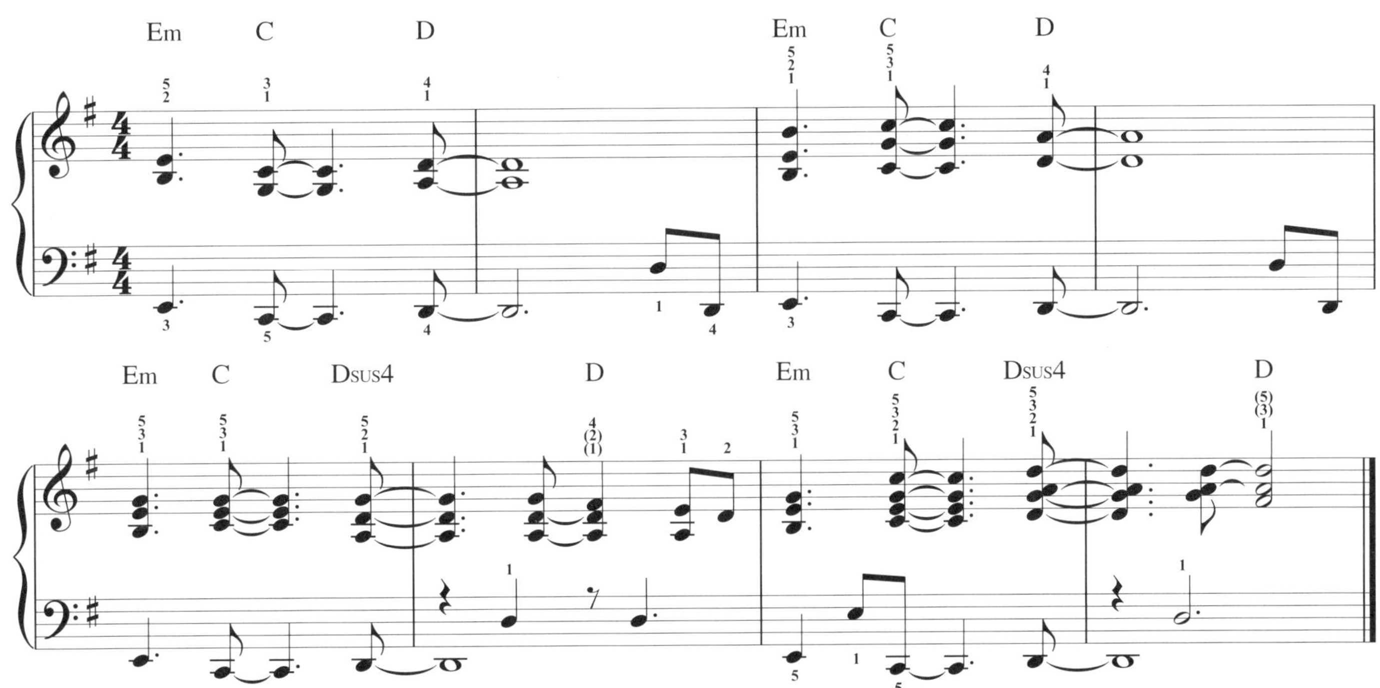

PROGRESSION 23

Song Reference: "Losing My Religion" by REM

Progression Tip: This chord progression is made up almost entirely of minor chords. The "Rhythmic Style" music contains lots of rock-piano techniques, including breaking the chords into **arpeggios** and octave doubling in the right hand.

Basic Progression

Am
Em
Am
Em
Dm
G
Am
Em

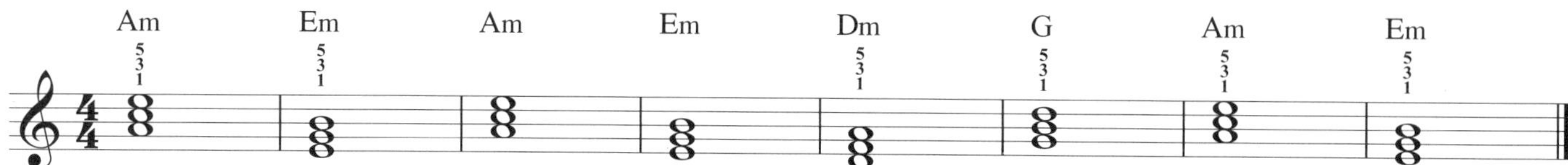

Rhythmic Style: Rock

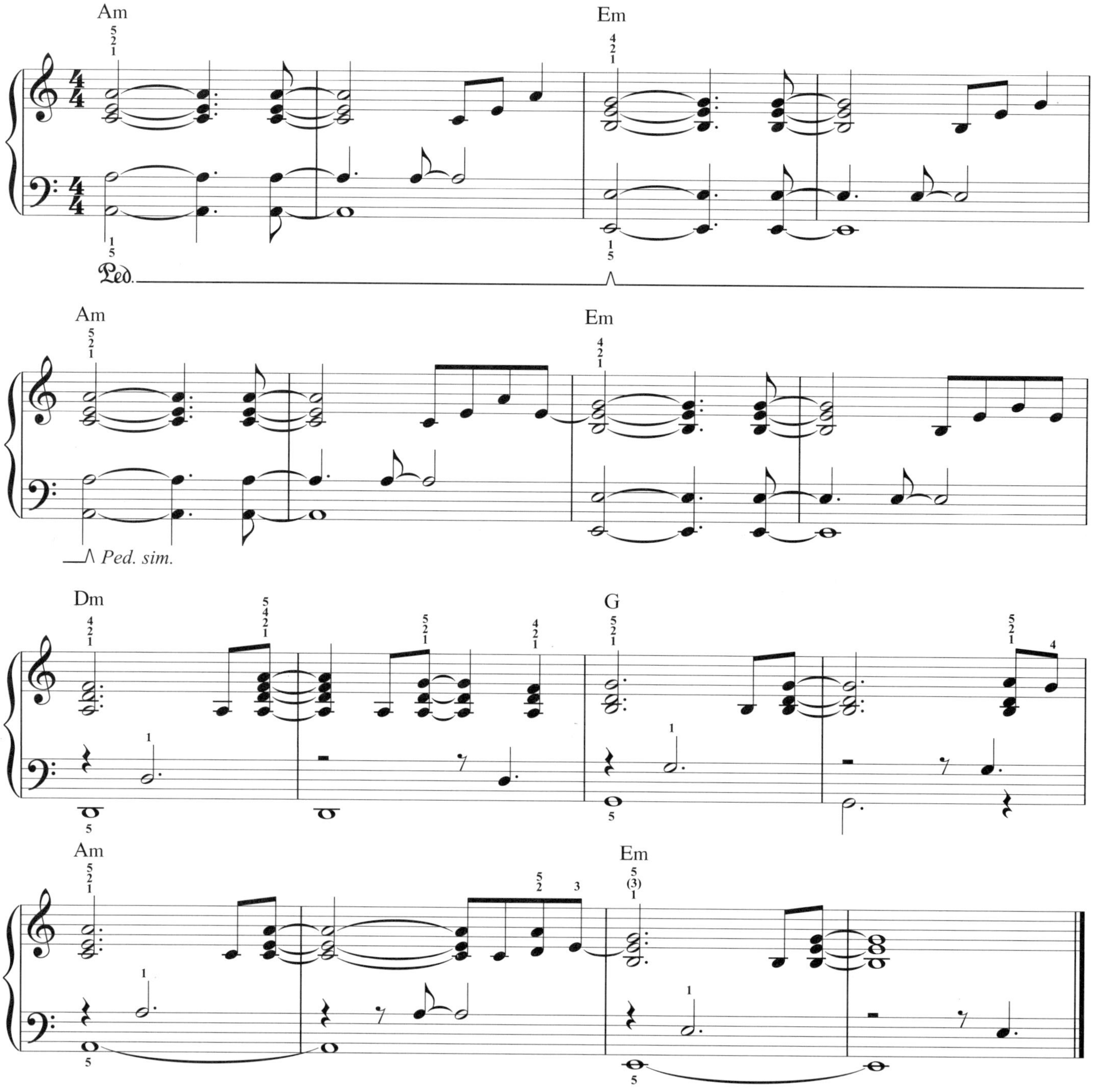
Am
Em
Ped.
Am
Em
Ped. sim.
Dm
G
Am
Em

PROGRESSION 24

Song Reference: "Mad World" by Tears for Fears

Progression Tip: This chord progression is in the key of F minor but uses a major version of chord IV, B-flat major. (Normally chord iv in a minor key is also minor.) This "major-minor mix" is quite a common technique in progressive rock chord progressions.

Basic Progression

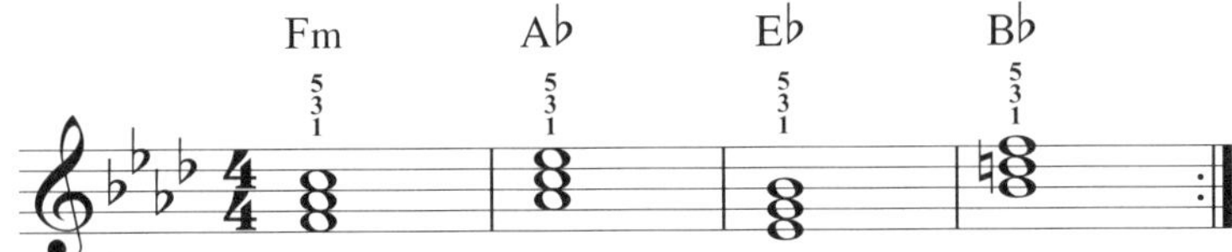

Rhythmic Style: Progressive Rock

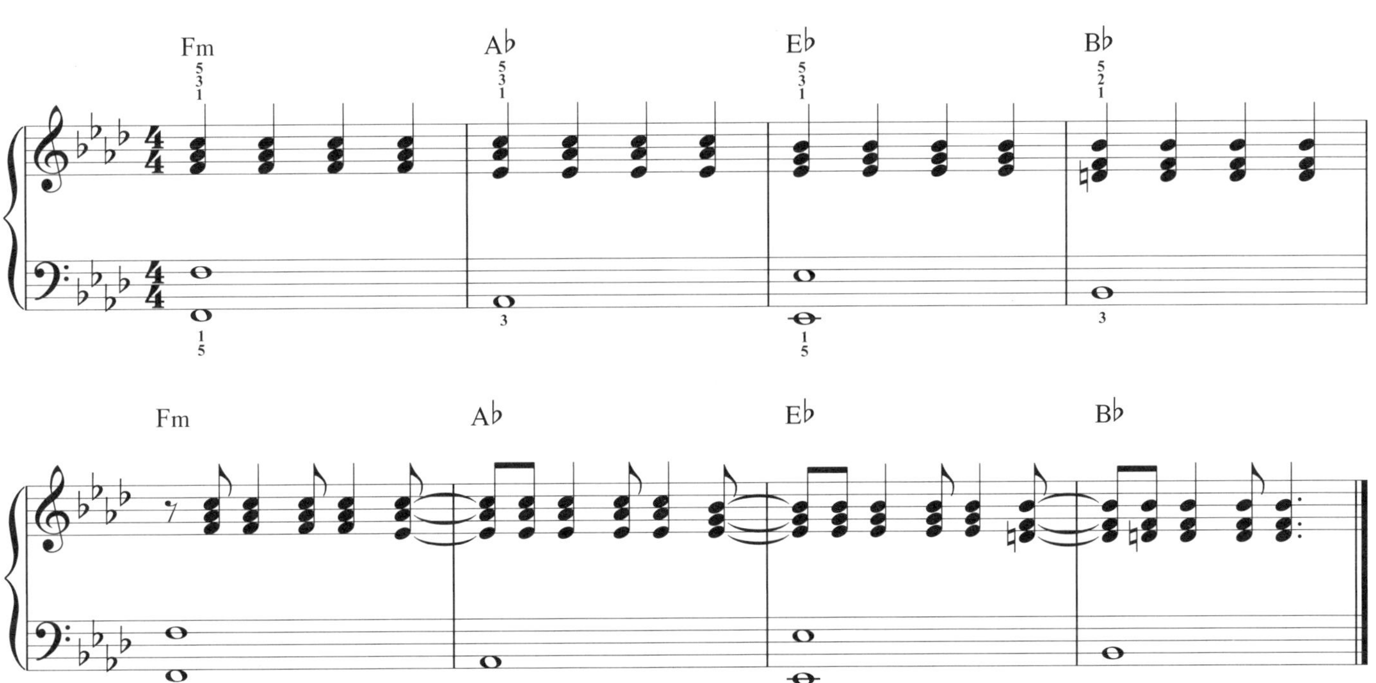

SIMPLE CIRCLE PROGRESSIONS

PROGRESSION 25

Song Reference: "Addicted to Love" by Robert Palmer

Progression Tip: This chord progression involves a **circle pattern**. Circle patterns are a common technique in popular chord progressions. Following an initial chord of A, this progression involves a two-chord pattern that outlines a IV–I movement. This is called a **circle of 4ths**. (G–D is a **IV–I** in D, then D–A is a **IV–I** in A.)

Basic Progression

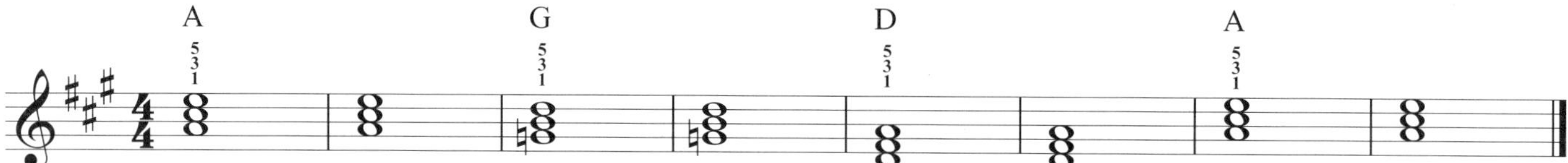

Rhythmic Style: Classic Rock

PROGRESSION 26

Song Reference: "Hey Joe" by Jimi Hendrix

Progression Tip: A longer circle of 4ths pattern is seen here starting on C, (C-G-D-A-E). The "Rhythmic Style" music shows us some piano ballad playing, with the right hand alternating between notes of the triad during beats 2 and 4.

Basic Progression

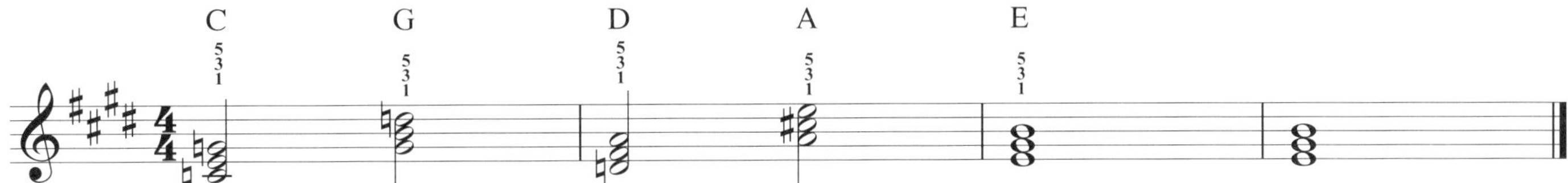

Rhythmic Style: Rock Ballad

PROGRESSION 27

Song Reference: "Jumping Jack Flash" by The Rolling Stones

Progression Tip: This B major progression begins on a D chord, before moving through the circle of 4ths technique as we've been exploring previously.

Basic Progression

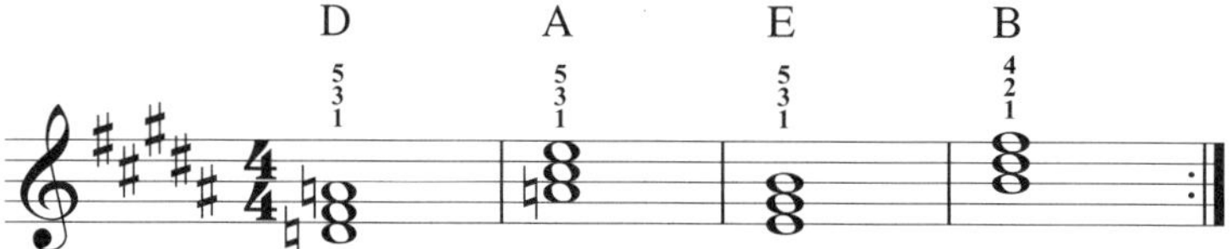

Rhythmic Style: Classic Rock

PROGRESSION 28

Song Reference: "And She Was" by Talking Heads

Progression Tip: Here we explore a new circle pattern, the **circle of 5ths**. (E–A is a **V–I** in A, A–D is a **V–I** in D.) The second half of the progression highlights our circle of 4ths. (D–A is a **IV–I** in A, A–E on the repeat is a **IV–I** in E.) Notice the concerted rhythm again for the "Rhythmic Style" music, giving a typical rock feel.

Basic Progression

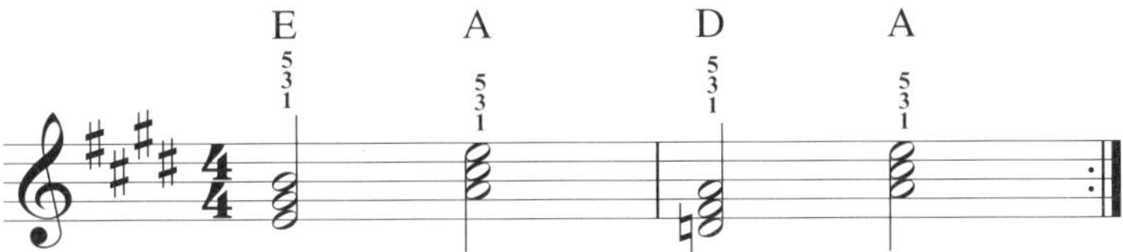

Rhythmic Style: Rock

PROGRESSION 29

Song Reference: "Don't You (Forget About Me)" by Simple Minds

Progression Tip: After an initial F major chord, this progression moves to E-flat major and a combination of the two types of circle progression previously learned.

Basic Progression

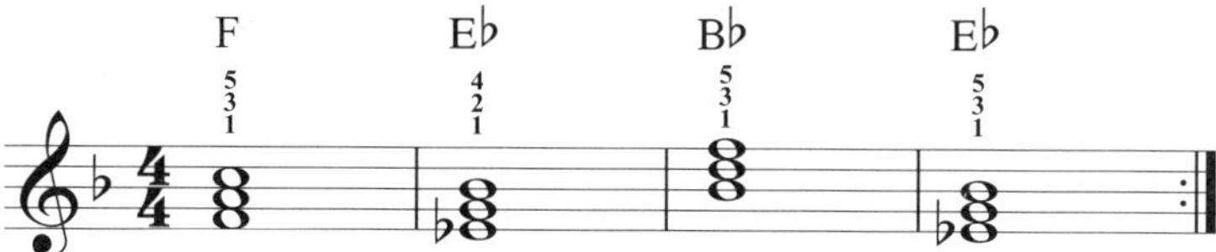

Rhythmic Style: Pop-Rock

PROGRESSIONS WITH SEVENTH CHORDS

PROGRESSION 30

Song Reference: "Killing Me Softly with His Song" by Roberta Flack

Progression Tip: From now on, progressions will involve **extended chords** (chords that contain at least four different notes). Mostly, the extra fourth note will be a seventh above the root of the chord. (E.g., G, B, D, **F** = G7.) These are called **seventh chords**.

Basic Progression

PROGRESSION 31

Song Reference: "We've Only Just Begun" by the Carpenters

Progression Tip: The progressions now start to combine our previously learned "sus" and "seventh" chords into one. Such chords replace the usual third with the fourth (the "sus" bit) while also adding a seventh. (E.g., "E7sus4" is E-**A**-B-D.)

Basic Progression

Amaj7
Dmaj7
C♯m7
F♯m7
Bm7
F♯m7
Bm7
E7sus4
E7

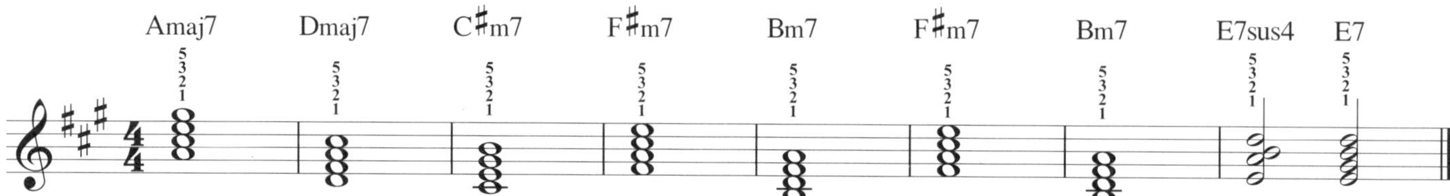

Rhythmic Style: Pop Ballad

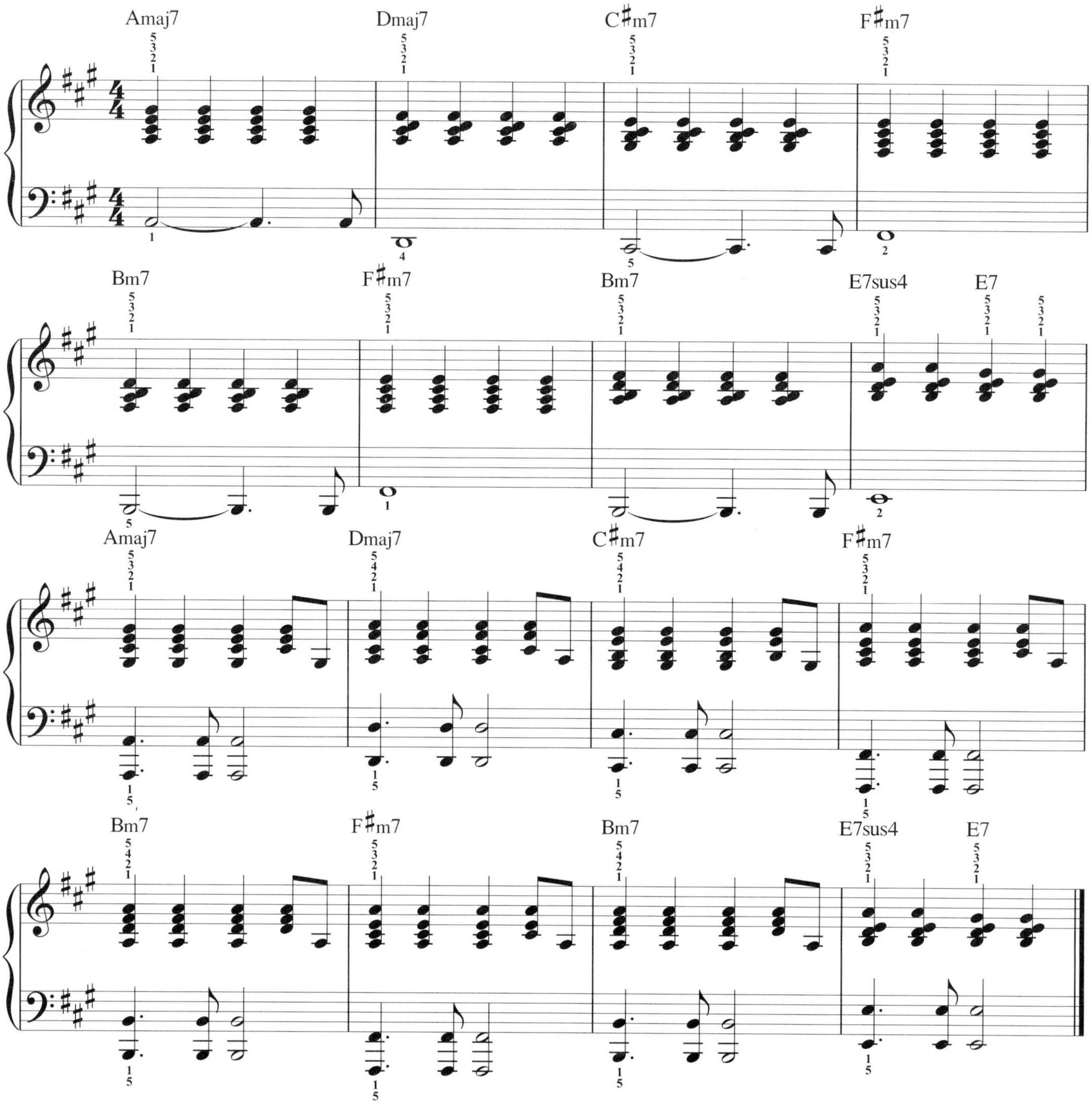

Amaj7
Dmaj7
C♯m7
F♯m7
Bm7
F♯m7
Bm7
E7sus4
E7
Amaj7
Dmaj7
C♯m7
F♯m7
Bm7
F♯m7
Bm7
E7sus4
E7

PROGRESSION 32

Song Reference: "Have I Told You Lately" by Van Morrison

Progression Tip: The learned "7sus4" chord (here, on B) has been revoiced in the "Rhythmic Style" music. In basic terms, it has become an A major right-hand triad with a B in the left-hand bass. This creates a sound that is common across a range of contemporary pop and R&B styles. We also see the common "splitting off" method of playing. Here, the root is in the left hand and the remaining notes in the right hand. Playing chords like this gives a cleaner and more professional sound to progressions.

Basic Progression

Emaj7
G♯m7
Amaj7
B7sus4

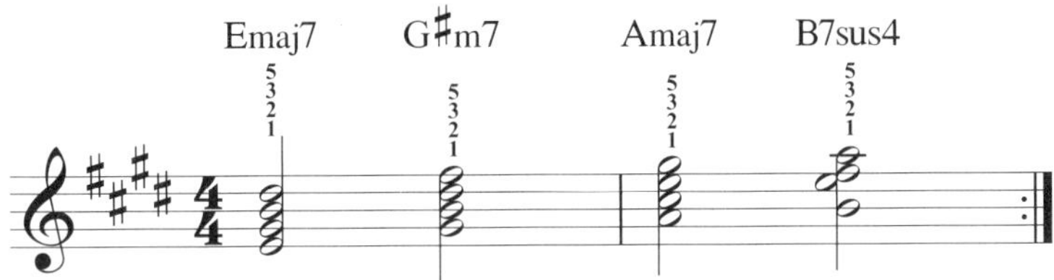

Rhythmic Style: R&B

Emaj7
G♯m7
Amaj7
B7sus4
Emaj7
G♯m7
Ped.
Ped. sim.
Amaj7
B7sus4
Emaj7
G♯m7
Amaj7
B7sus4
Emaj7
G♯m7
Amaj7
B7sus4

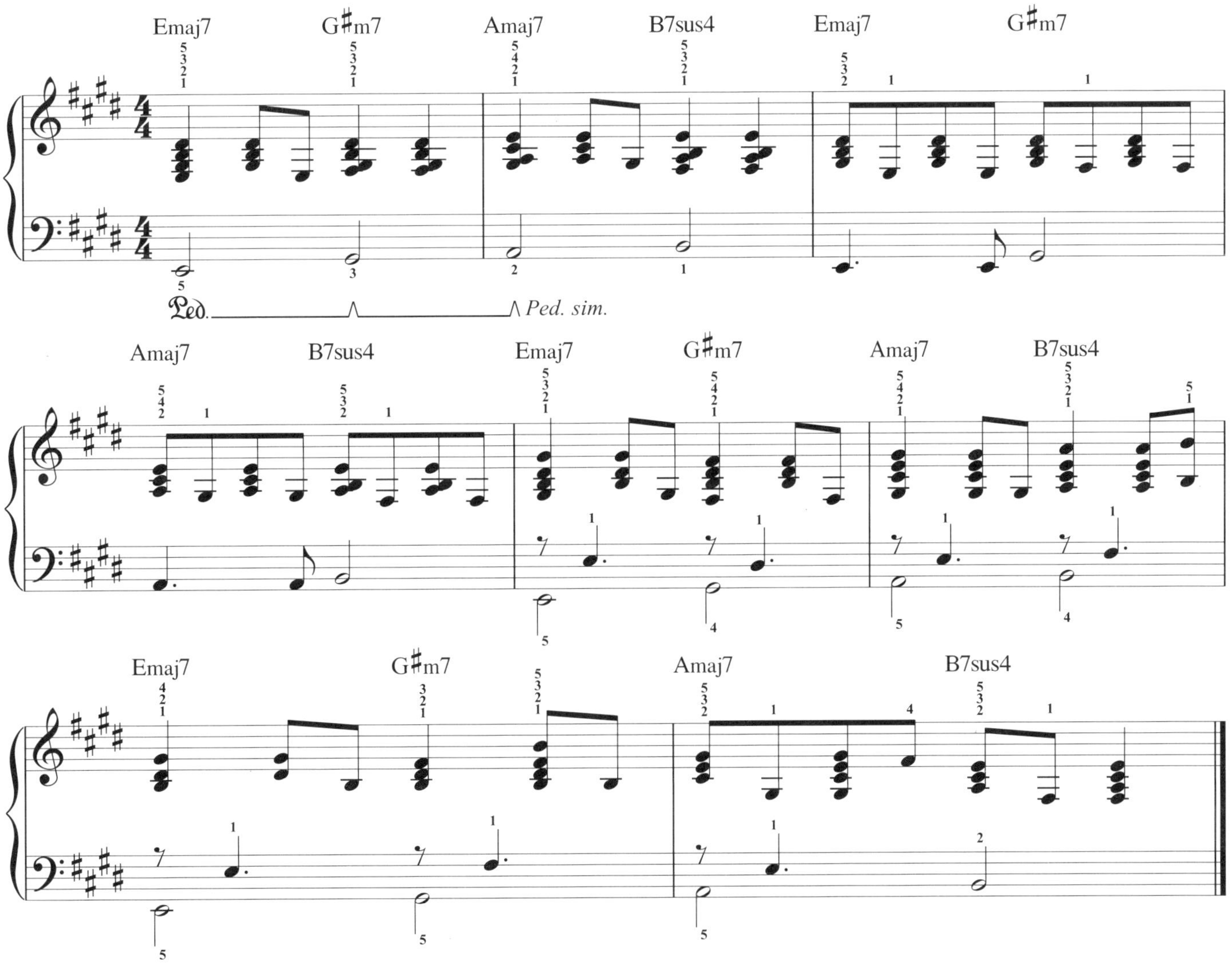

PROGRESSION 33

Song Reference: "Saving All My Love for You" by Whitney Houston

Progression Tip: The chords in this progression are written out using the two types of voicing learned; basic four-part chord spellings and "splitting off." Using both gives a smooth flow and authentic style to playing chord progressions.

Basic Progression

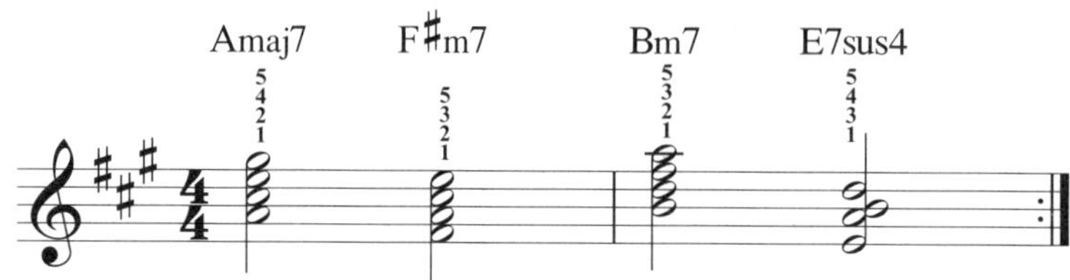

Rhythmic Style: Pop Ballad

Amaj7 F♯m7 Bm7 E7sus4 Amaj7 F♯m7

Ped. Ped. sim.

Bm7 E7sus4 Amaj7 F♯m7 Bm7 E7sus4

Amaj7 F♯m7 Bm7 E7sus4

PROGRESSION 34

Song Reference: "The Greatest Love of All" by Whitney Houston

Progression Tip: All chords in this progression are "split off," giving a sophistication and movement to the music. The root of each chord also highlights a simple circle progression.

Basic Progression

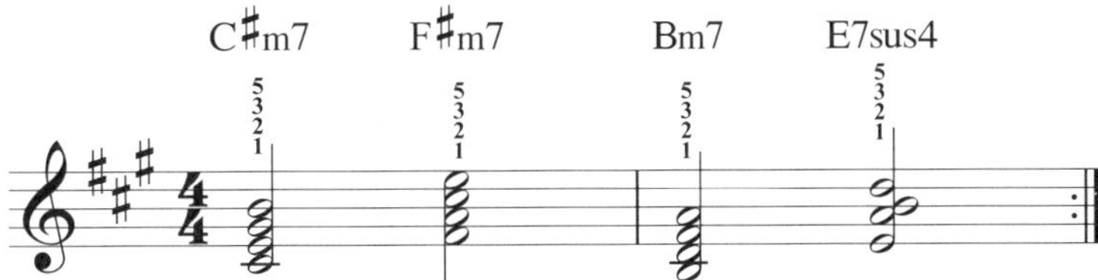

Rhythmic Style: Pop

C♯m7 F♯m7 Bm7 E7sus4 C♯m7 F♯m7

Ped. Ped. sim.

Bm7 E7sus4 C♯m7 F♯m7 Bm7 E7sus4

C♯m7 F♯m7 Bm7 E7sus4

PROGRESSION 35

Song Reference: "Let's Stay Together" by Al Green

Progression Tip: Note how the left hand gradually builds up in intensity during the "Rhythmic Style" progression, using shorter note values. In this R&B progression, the first right-hand D minor triad (D, F, A) is built from the third of the overall B-flat major seventh chord (B♭, **D**, F, A). This is known as utilizing **upper structures**. In upper structures, the right-hand chord forms a triad built from a note in the prevailing harmony.

Basic Progression

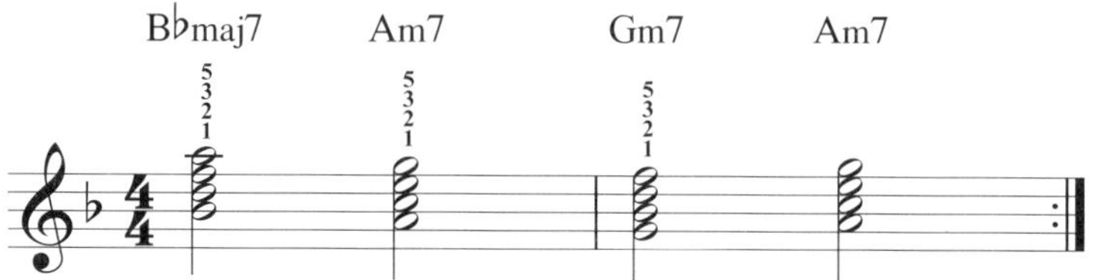

Rhythmic Style: R&B

PROGRESSION 36

Song Reference: "Minute by Minute" by The Doobie Brothers

Progression Tip: This progression involves mixing together our seventh and "sus" seventh chords together, in the key of C. The voicing of the chords in the "Rhythmic Style" music are quite advanced, adding a sophisticated professionalism to the progression.

Basic Progression

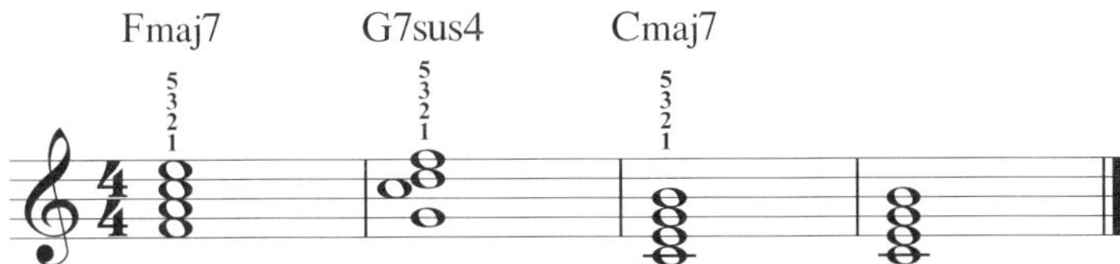

Rhythmic Style: R&B

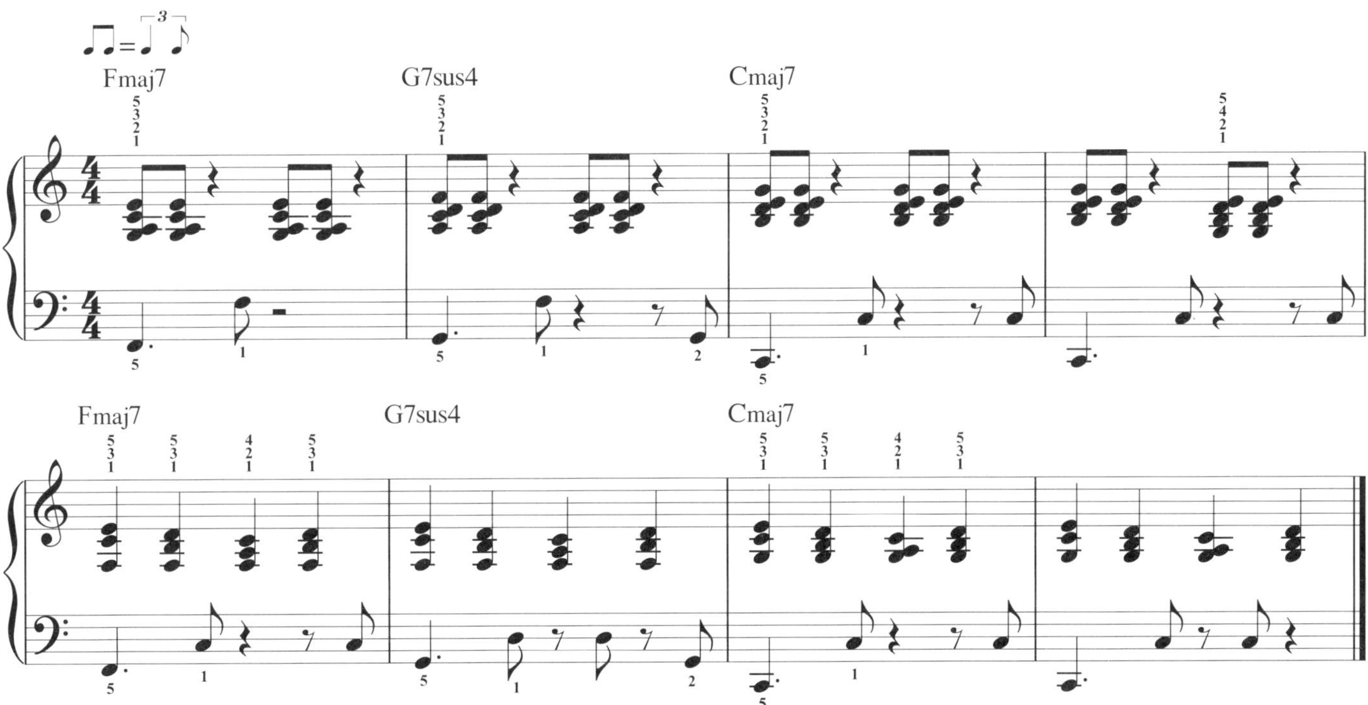

PROGRESSION 37

Song Reference: "Careless Whisper" by George Michael

Progression Tip: So far, the seventh chords used have been based on major keys. Seventh chords in minor keys will now appear in some of the following progressions.

Basic Progression

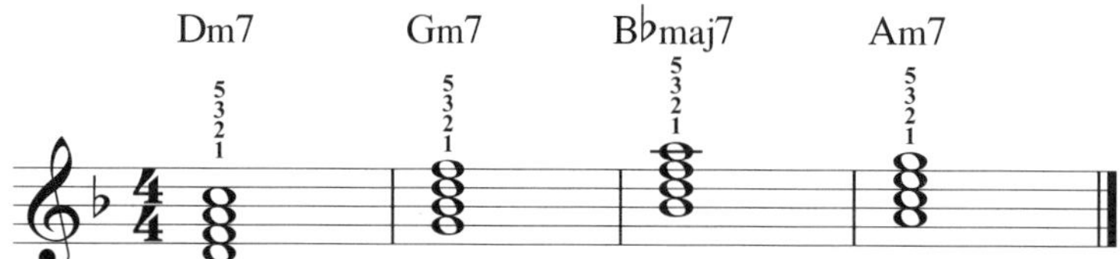

Rhythmic Style: R&B/Pop Ballad

PROGRESSION 38

Song Reference: "Ain't No Sunshine" by Bill Withers

Progression Tip: This progression is made up exclusively of minor seventh chords. In the R&B styling, upper structures dominate the voicing while rests add gentle syncopation to the groove.

Basic Progression

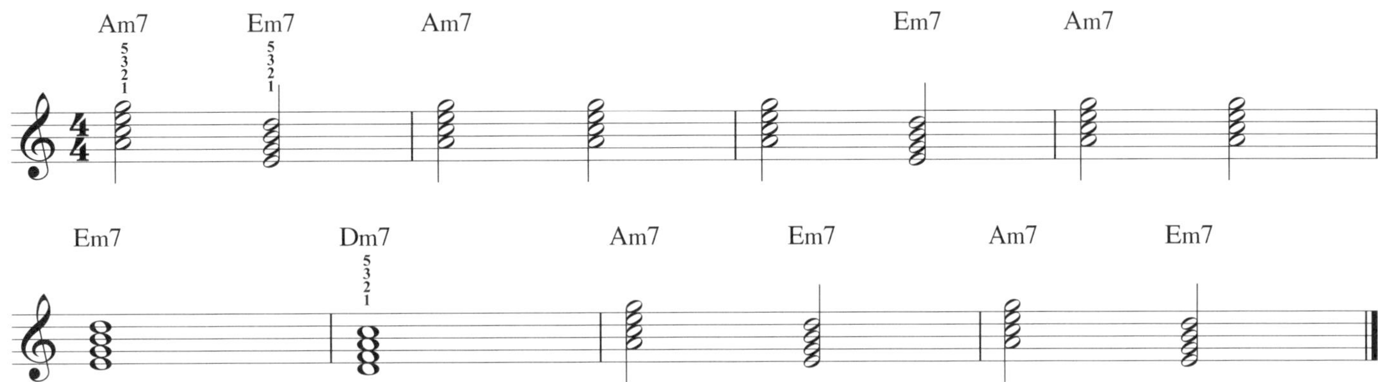

Rhythmic Style: R&B

PROGRESSION 39

Song Reference: "I Will Survive" by Gloria Gaynor

Progression Tip: The voicings in this progression are just simple, four-part chord spellings, allowing some focus on the new minor seventh (♭5) chord being used.

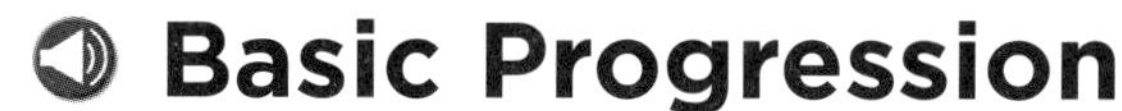

Basic Progression

Am7
Dm7
G7
Cmaj7
Fmaj7
Bm7♭5
E7sus4
E7

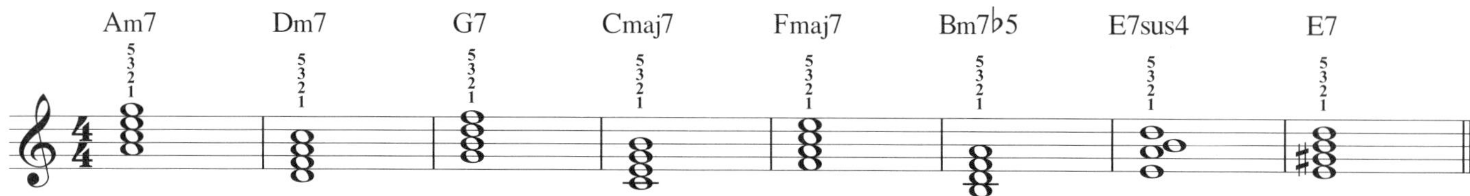

Rhythmic Style: Disco

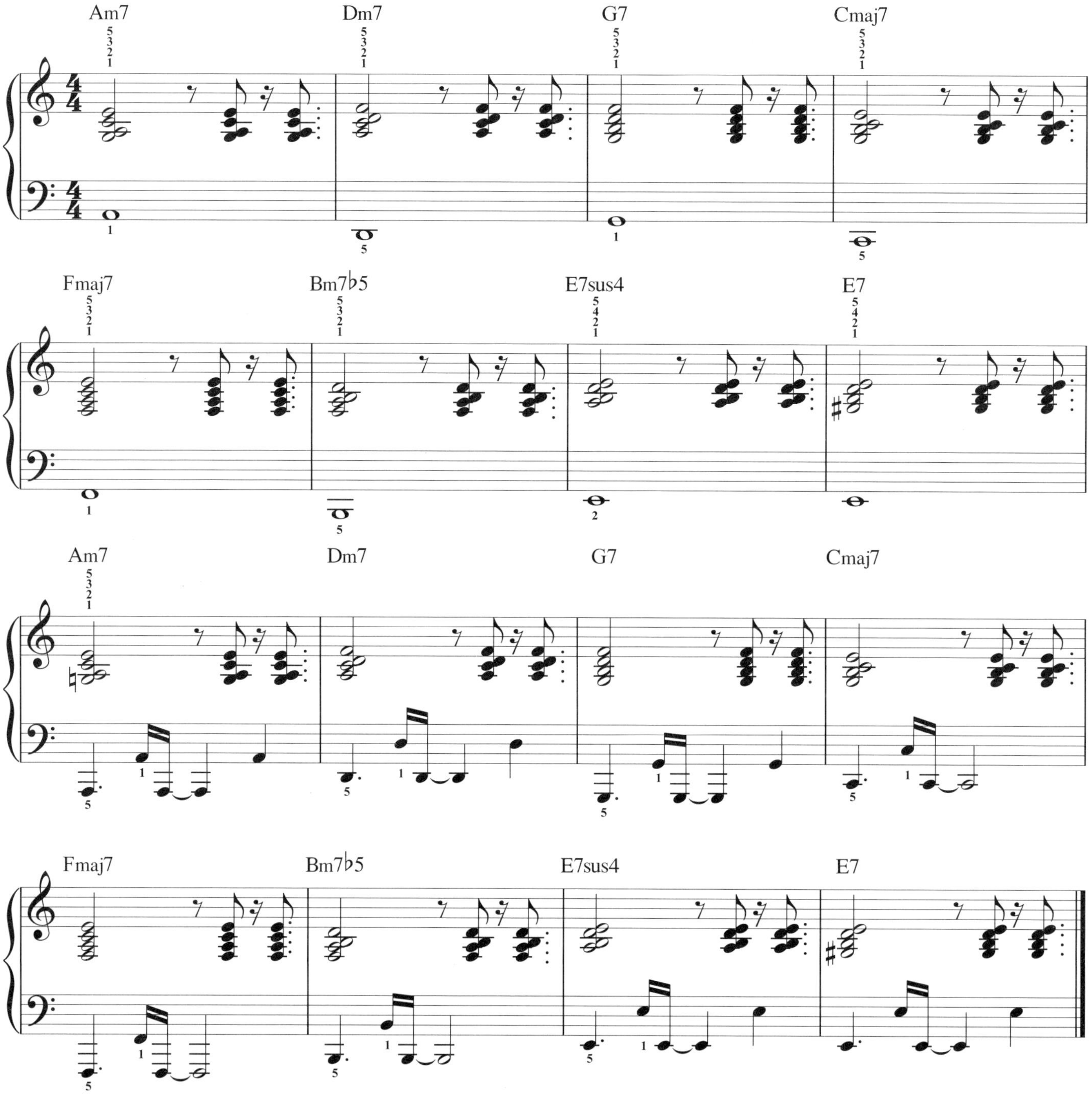

Am7
Dm7
G7
Cmaj7
Fmaj7
Bm7♭5
E7sus4
E7
Am7
Dm7
G7
Cmaj7
Fmaj7
Bm7♭5
E7sus4
E7

MORE ADVANCED PROGRESSIONS

PROGRESSION 40

Song Reference: "Don't Know Why" by Norah Jones

Progression Tip: This chord progression uses lots of **accidentals** (sharp, flat, or natural symbols). This is because some chords have notes that do not belong to the overall key of the music (**chromatic** notes). It also introduces an altered dominant chord: the D7♯9. In the first half of this example, we're playing the seventh and third of each chord in the right hand, sometimes over root-seventh intervals in the left hand. This type of "seven-three" voicing is a staple sound in jazz-style progressions.

Basic Progression

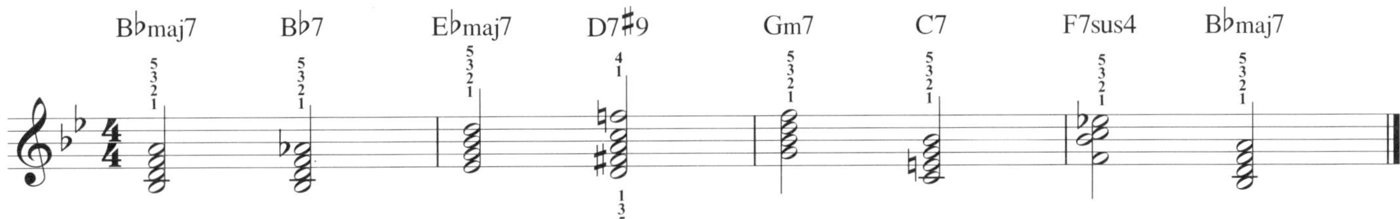

Rhythmic Style: Jazz Ballad

PROGRESSION 41

Song Reference: "Holding Back the Years" by Simply Red

Progression Tip: Here, we encounter a five-note chord for a ii–V progression in D-flat major. The number "9" by a chord shows it uses notes a seventh and a ninth above the root. E.g., A♭9 contains the triad A-flat–C–E-flat, plus G-flat (7th), and B-flat (9th). As chords become larger, they are increasingly less likely to be played exactly as they are spelled. Here, upper-structure triads and four-part chords are used for a smoother, more professional sound.

Basic Progression

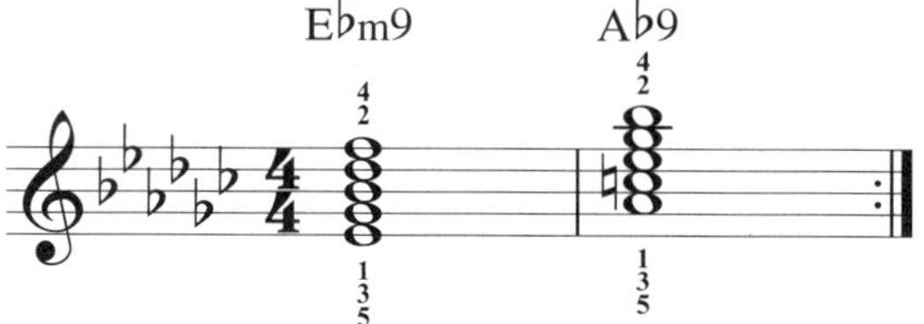

Rhythmic Style: Pop

PROGRESSION 42

Song Reference: "After the Love Has Gone" by Earth, Wind & Fire

Progression Tip: This progression is in A-flat major but uses the technique of borrowing chords from another key. Here, measures 3–4 use chromatic chords, taken from the key of G-flat major. In this key, the chords make up a standard ii–V–I progression. This is a common technique in popular music styles, used to generate added interest.

Basic Progression

Cm7 Fm7 B♭m7 E♭7sus4 A♭m7 D♭7sus4 G♭maj7 A♭m7 B♭m7

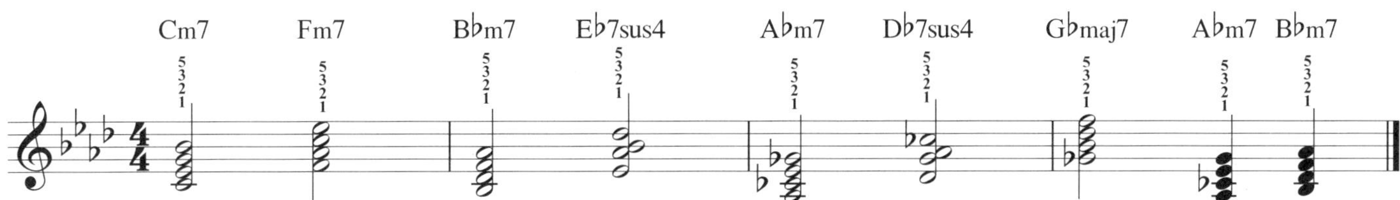

Rhythmic Style: R&B

Cm7 Fm7 B♭m7 E♭7sus4 A♭m7 D♭7sus4 G♭maj7 A♭m7 B♭m7
Ped. Ped. sim.
Cm7 Fm7 B♭m7 E♭7sus4
A♭m7 D♭7sus4 G♭maj7 A♭m7 B♭m7

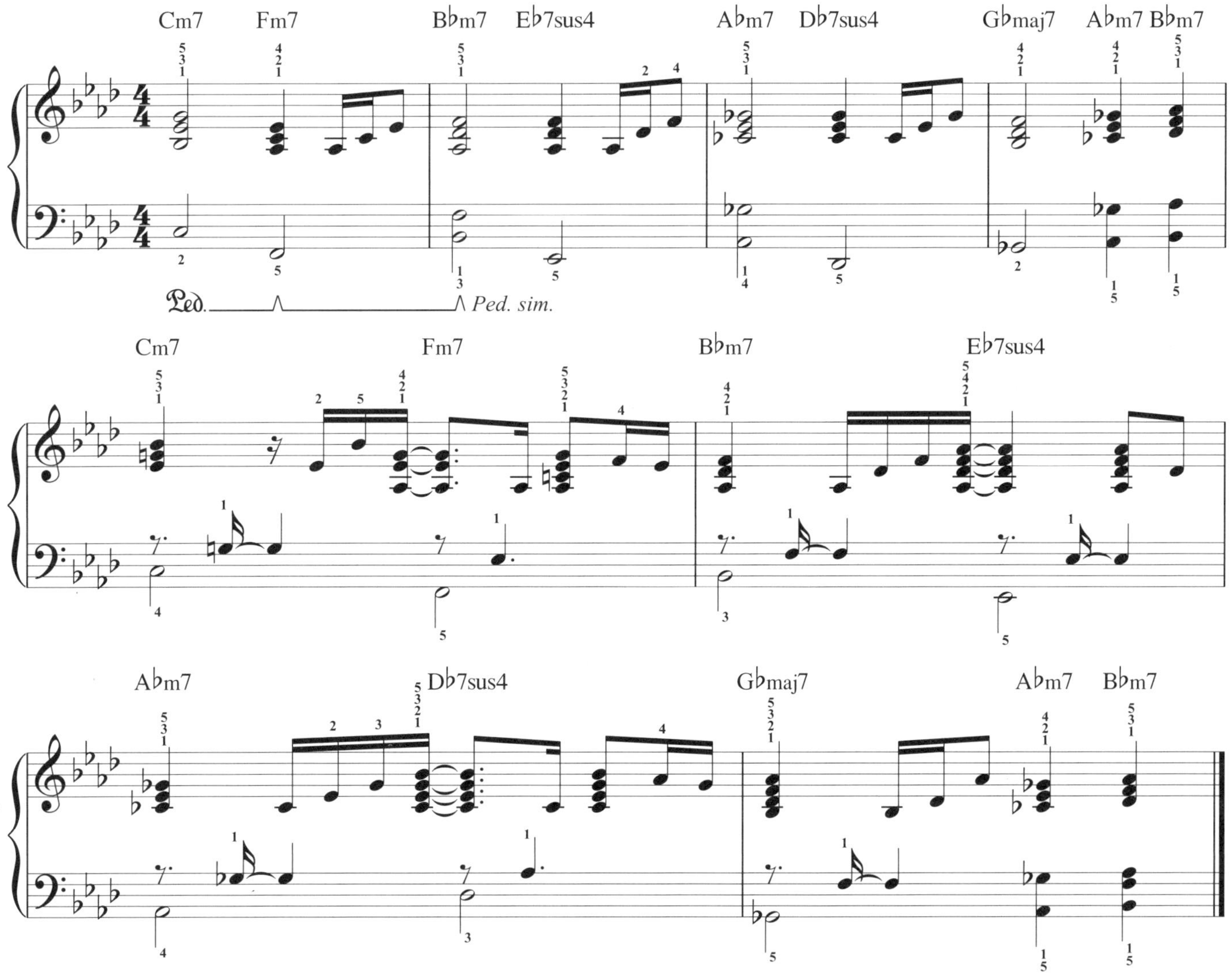

PROGRESSION 43

Song Reference: "Autumn Leaves" by Joseph Kosma

Progression Tip: This uses the "ii–V–I progression" in two different keys, G major and E minor. These two keys share the same key signature; in other words, they are **relative** to one another.

Basic Progression

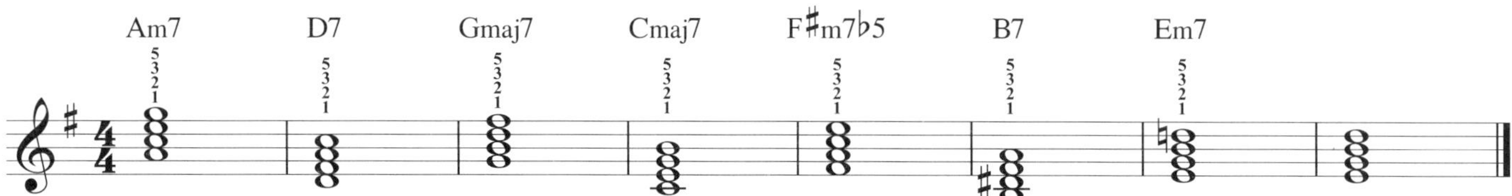

Rhythmic Style: Jazz Standard

PROGRESSION 44

Song Reference: "Misty" by Erroll Garner

Progression Tip: This progression uses a lot of our more advanced techniques, including upper structures and the ii–V–I movement from a different key.

Basic Progression

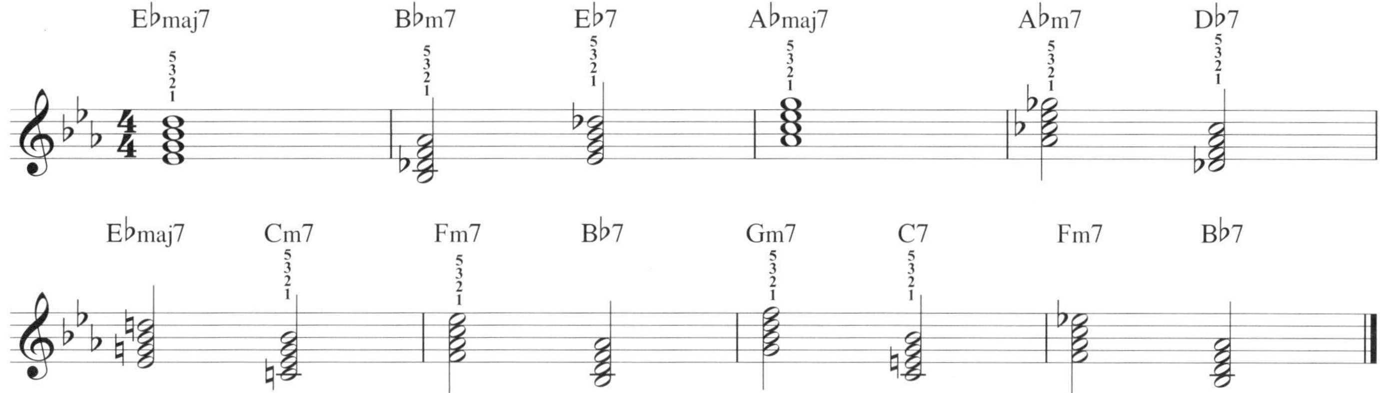

Rhythmic Style: Jazz Ballad

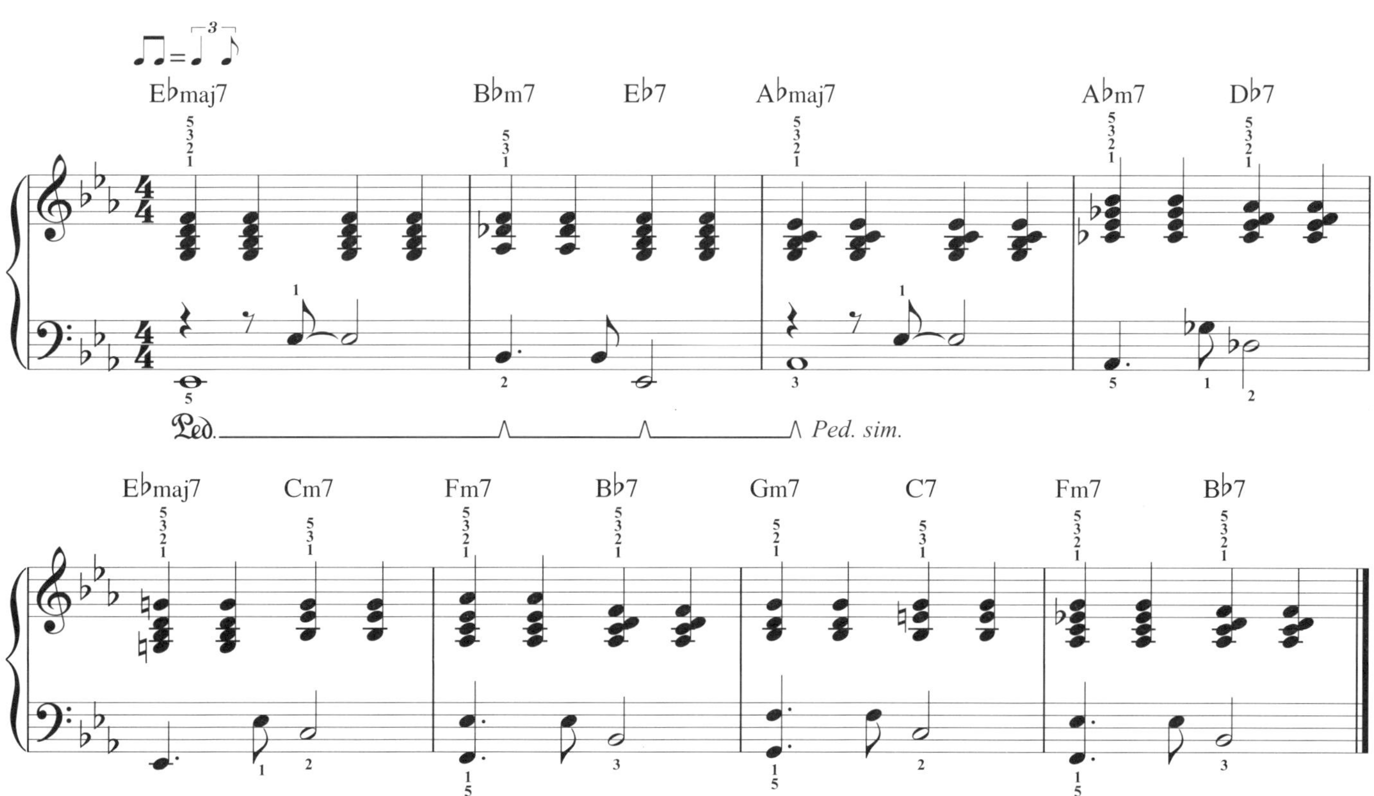

PROGRESSION 45

Song Reference: "Get Back" by The Beatles

Progression Tip: This progression uses **dominant seventh** chords. Although these resolve back to chord I in the majority of styles (e.g., G7 moving to C), in blues progressions we often find them occurring from the first, fourth, and/or fifth notes of the scale. The left-hand pattern in this "Rhythmic Style" music is typical of pop and rock piano playing.

Basic Progression

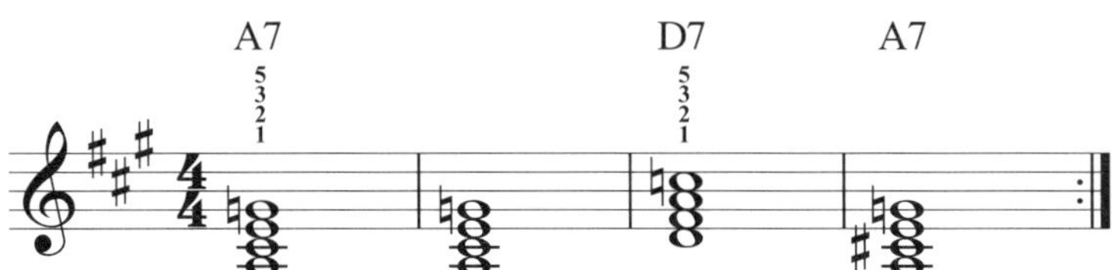

Rhythmic Style: Blues-Rock

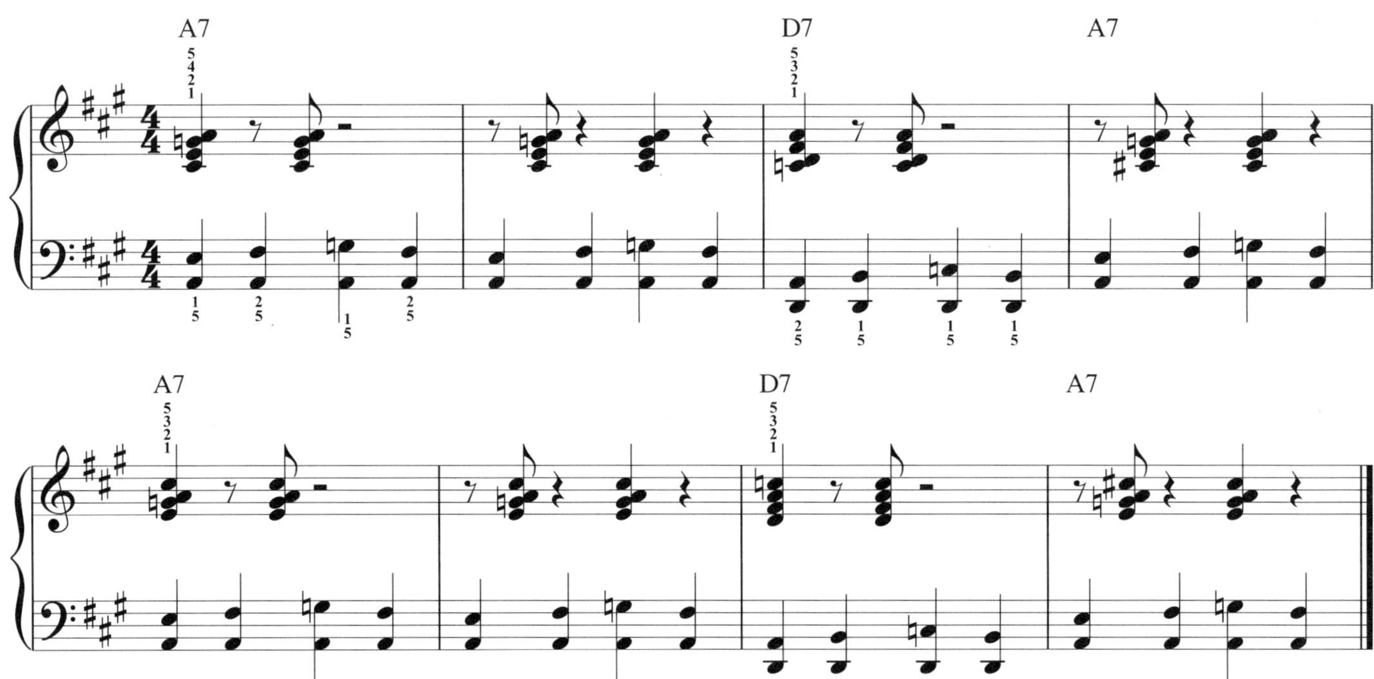

PROGRESSION 46

Song Reference: "Spinning Wheel" by Blood, Sweat & Tears

Progression Tip: In this progression, dominant sevenths are joined together in a circle of 5ths pattern, a common chord sequence in popular music.

Basic Progression

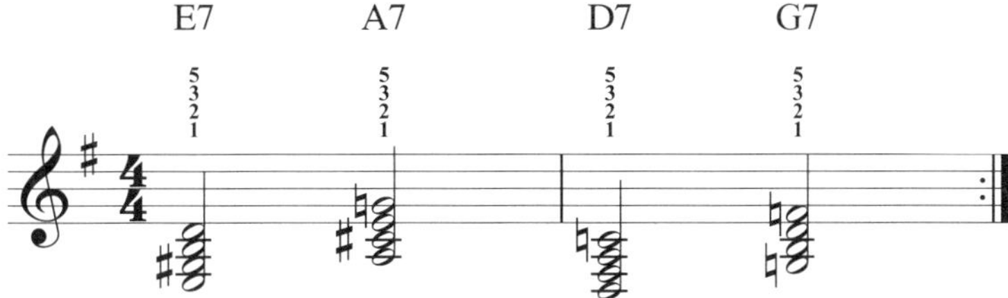

Rhythmic Style: R&B

PROGRESSION 47

Song Reference: "Takin' Care of Business" by Bachman-Turner Overdrive

Progression Tip: This typical rock-blues progression uses various dominant seventh chords. The "Rhythmic Style" music uses two different right-hand techniques; the first half sees inversions of dominant seventh chords while the second uses root–fifth voicings in a style typical of rock 'n' roll piano.

Basic Progression

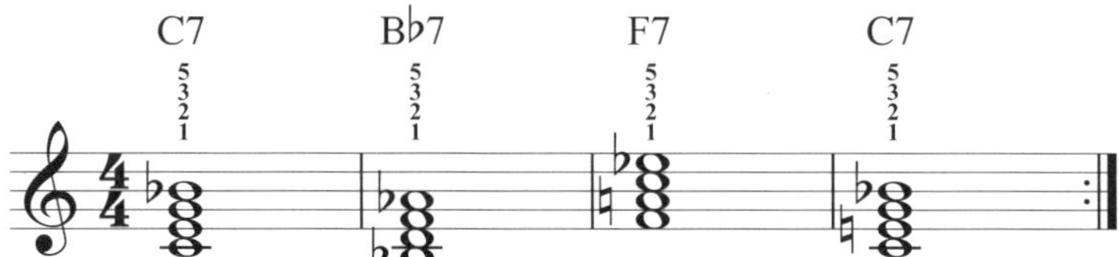

Rhythmic Style: Blues-Rock

C7 B♭7 F7 C7

B♭7 F7 C7

B♭7 F7 C7

B♭7 F7 C7

PROGRESSION 48

Song Reference: "What You Won't Do for Love" by Bobby Caldwell

Progression Tip: Here, the progression encounters chord symbols with a number "13." These chords include the notes that are a seventh, ninth, and thirteenth above the root! As with before, the technique of "borrowing" from other keys is shown in this progression. For example, the final two chords form a ii–V progression in E.

Basic Progression

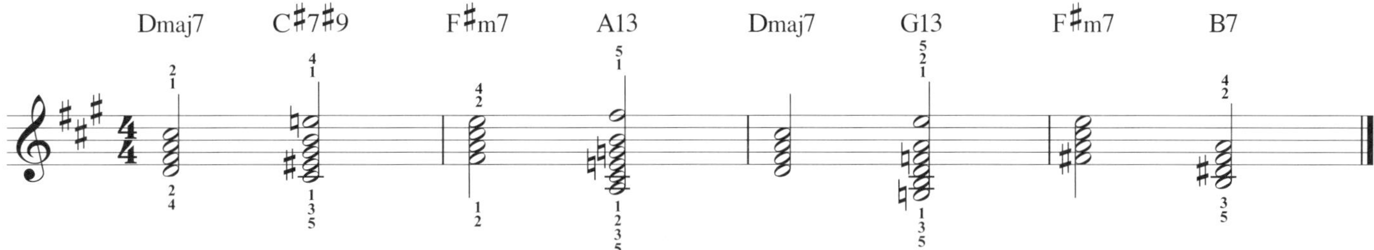

Rhythmic Style: Funk

PROGRESSION 49

Song Reference: "All Blues" by Miles Davis

Progression Tip: In this progression, the right hand is using notes outside of the chord symbol entirely. Jazz pianists often use notes in their chord progressions that are taken from different types of scales, known as **modes**. In the "Rhythmic Style" music, right-hand notes above the G7 chord are taken from the **G Mixolydian** mode. Their use in third intervals is a classic jazz and blues technique for this type of progression.

Basic Progression

Rhythmic Style: Jazz and Blues

PROGRESSION 50

Song Reference: "Freddie Freeloader" by Miles Davis

Progression Tip: Here, we have extended thirteenth chords and right-hand triads using notes from the Mixolydian mode. Progressions of this type are important tools in sophisticated jazz, blues, funk, and gospel styles.

Basic Progression

B♭13
E♭13
B♭13
F7
E♭7
A♭9

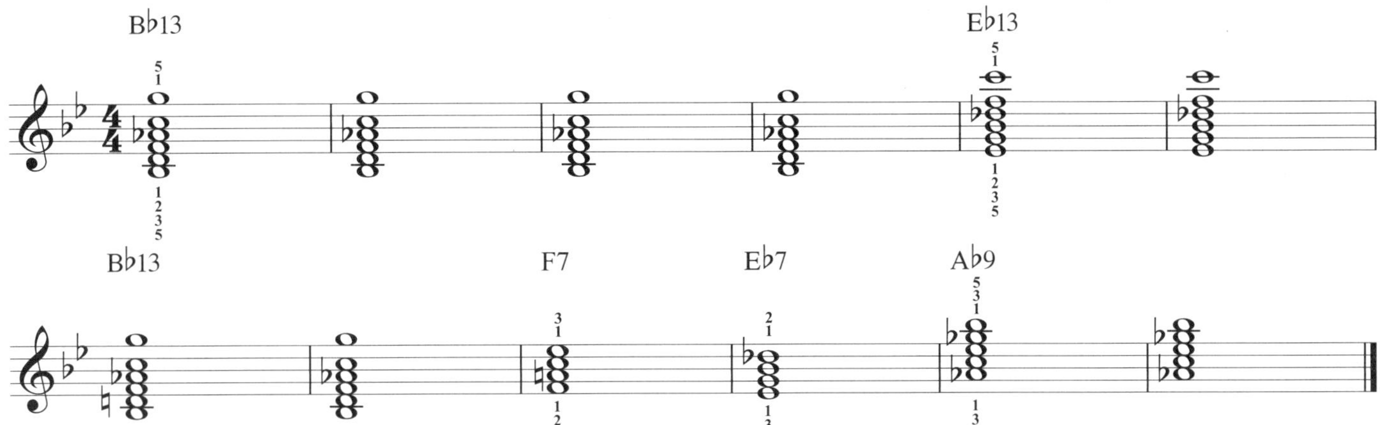

Rhythmic Style: Jazz

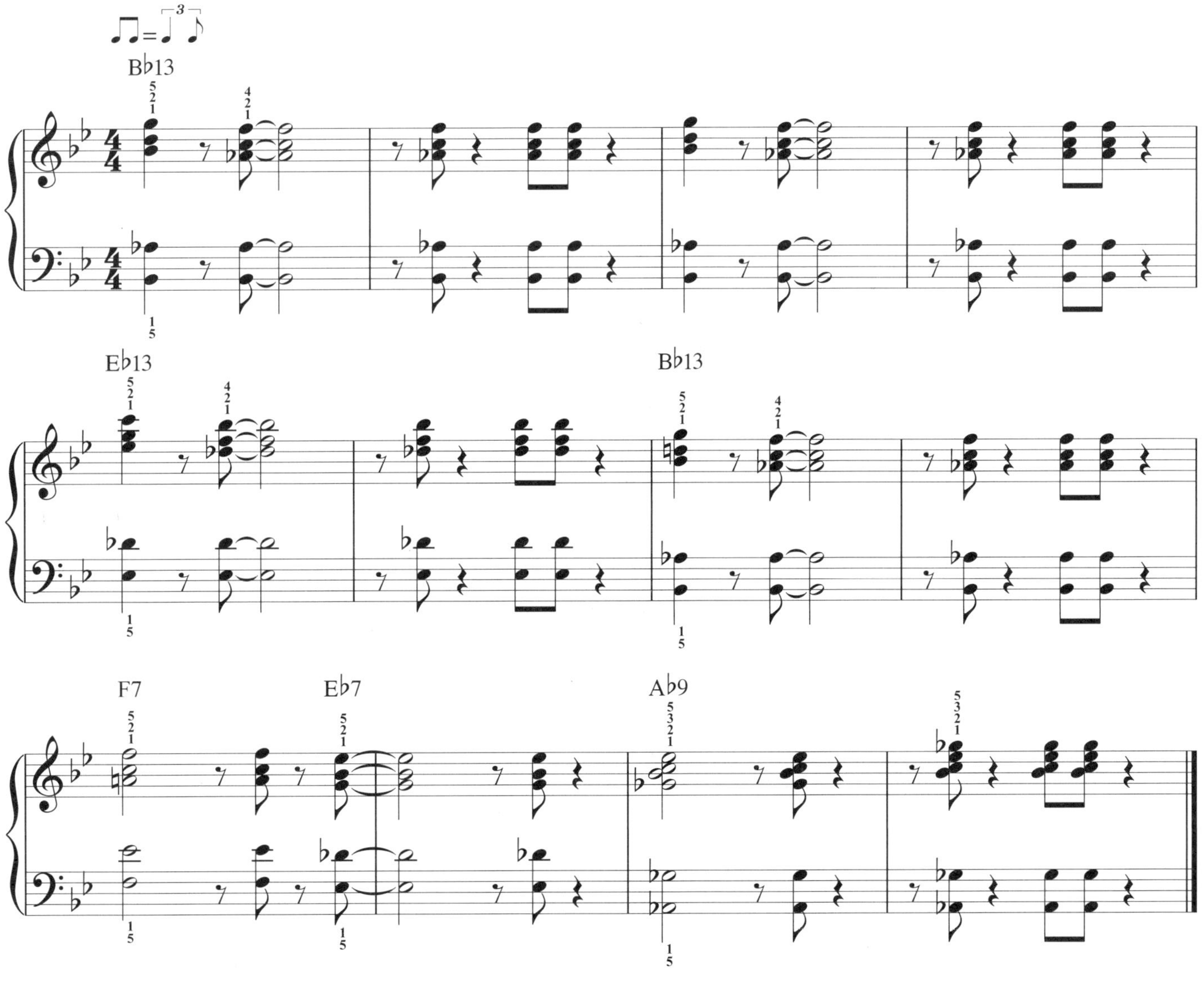

B♭13
E♭13
B♭13
F7
E♭7
A♭9

ABOUT THE AUTHOR

Mark Harrison is a professional keyboardist, composer, arranger, author, and music educator based in Los Angeles. He has recorded three albums as a contemporary jazz bandleader with the Mark Harrison Quintet, and performs regularly throughout southern California with the Steely Dan tribute band Doctor Wu. Mark's TV music credits include "Saturday Night Live," "American Justice," "Celebrity Profiles," "America's Most Wanted," "True Hollywood Stories," and many others. Mark is an endorsed artist-educator for Dexibell keyboards, performing at the world-renowned NAMM music industry trade show in Los Angeles.

Mark has held faculty positions at the Grove School of Music and at the University of Southern California (Thornton School of Music). He runs a busy online teaching studio, catering to the needs of professional and aspiring musicians worldwide. Mark's students include GRAMMY Award® winners, hit songwriters, members of the Boston Pops and L.A. Philharmonic orchestras, and first-call touring musicians with major acts. He has written over 30 music instruction books, as well as various "Master Class" articles for *Keyboard Magazine* and other publications.

For further information on Mark's educational products and online lessons, please visit www.harrisonmusic.com.